CREATING A GREAT BANK

Achieving Superior Performance
After the Perfect Storm

JAY KALAWAR
ANDREW MUTCH
PAUL ALLEN

Creative Editors: Andrew Mutch

Jay Kalawar

Contact Information:

Aston Associates

100 Overlook Center, 2nd Floor

Princeton, New Jersey 08540

Tel +1 609 375 2122 Fax +1 609 375 2313

www.astonassociates.com

TABLE OF CONTENTS

Contents   *Page*

Contents   *Page*

Acknowledgements

To our clients for helping us evolve our thinking in tandem with industry developments. In particular, we are indebted to Bob Weber and John Koelmel of First Niagara Financial Group, Buffalo, New York; Ed O'Neal (in memoriam), Gail Kelly and David Gall of St. George Bank; Daniel Musson of Insurance Australia Group, Sydney, Australia; Tom Hollister of Citizens Bank, formerly of BankBoston; Oliver Waddell and Joe Campanella formerly of Star Banc Corporation (now U.S. Bancorp), Minneapolis, Minnesota; Don McNeill formerly of Country Banc Holding, Oklahoma; William Balderston, III formerly of Lincoln First, Rochester, New York; Richard Dahl formerly of Bank of Hawaii, Honolulu, Hawaii; Spence Eccles and Morgan Evans of First Security, Salt Lake City, Utah; Chuck Coltman formerly of Corestates, Philadelphia, Pennsylvania; Christopher J. Carey of City National, formerly of Corestates; Mac McDonald and Gaylon Layfield formerly of Signet, Richmond, Virginia; John L. Klinck, Jr. of Mellon Financial, formerly of Signet; and Eugene Montgomery and Albert Christman of Community Financial Insurance Center, Monroe, Louisiana.

To our former colleagues Oliver Sommer, Steinar Ryen, Jacqueline Corbelli, and Elizabeth Uehling for their contributions to originally published articles.

For our families: Sandra, Emma, Mark, Caroline, and Edward; Kay, Anuva, and Arjuna; Erica, Lila and Abigail—for their continued love and support.

About the Authors

Paul Allen is Chairman of Aston Associates and author of "Reengineering the Bank" (McGraw Hill, 1997). Mr. Allen was formerly one of the leading partners in the financial institutions practice of **McKinsey & Co.**, working both in the New York and European offices. Mr. Allen and his team of some of the most highly regarded professionals in the financial services community bring over three decades of experience to strategic design. He earned his MBA from the Harvard Business School, where he was a Harkness Fellow and Baker Scholar, and his MA in Law from Oxford University, England.

Jay Kalawar is President of Aston Associates. Mr. Kalawar specializes in strategically positioning banks for sustained growth and profitability through acquisitions and business process, human capital, IT and CRM design in commercial, retail, consumer lending, asset management, trust and private banking. Mr. Kalawar started working for Aston in 1993 and led major operational redesign engagements at US Regional Banks, leading to substantial increases in shareholder value. Prior to 1993, Mr. Kalawar led major design and change efforts at Federal Reserve Bank of San Francisco, **McKinsey & Co** and **Bank of Montreal**. He has earned his MBA from the Haas School of Business at the University of California, Berkeley, and his Bachelor of Engineering from the Indian Institute of Technology, Kanpur.

Andrew Mutch is Managing Director of Aston Associates with extensive experience in retail and commercial banking, asset management and insurance. Prior to joining Aston in 2004, he was with **Right Management Consultants**, specializing in merger integration and strategic planning in the financial services, pharmaceutical and other consumer product industries. Andy earned his MBA from the Fuqua School of Business at Duke University, specializing in finance and strategy, and holds a bachelor's degree in management science and economics from Cornell University. He is a frequent contributor to such publications as *American Banker* and *Retail Banker International*.

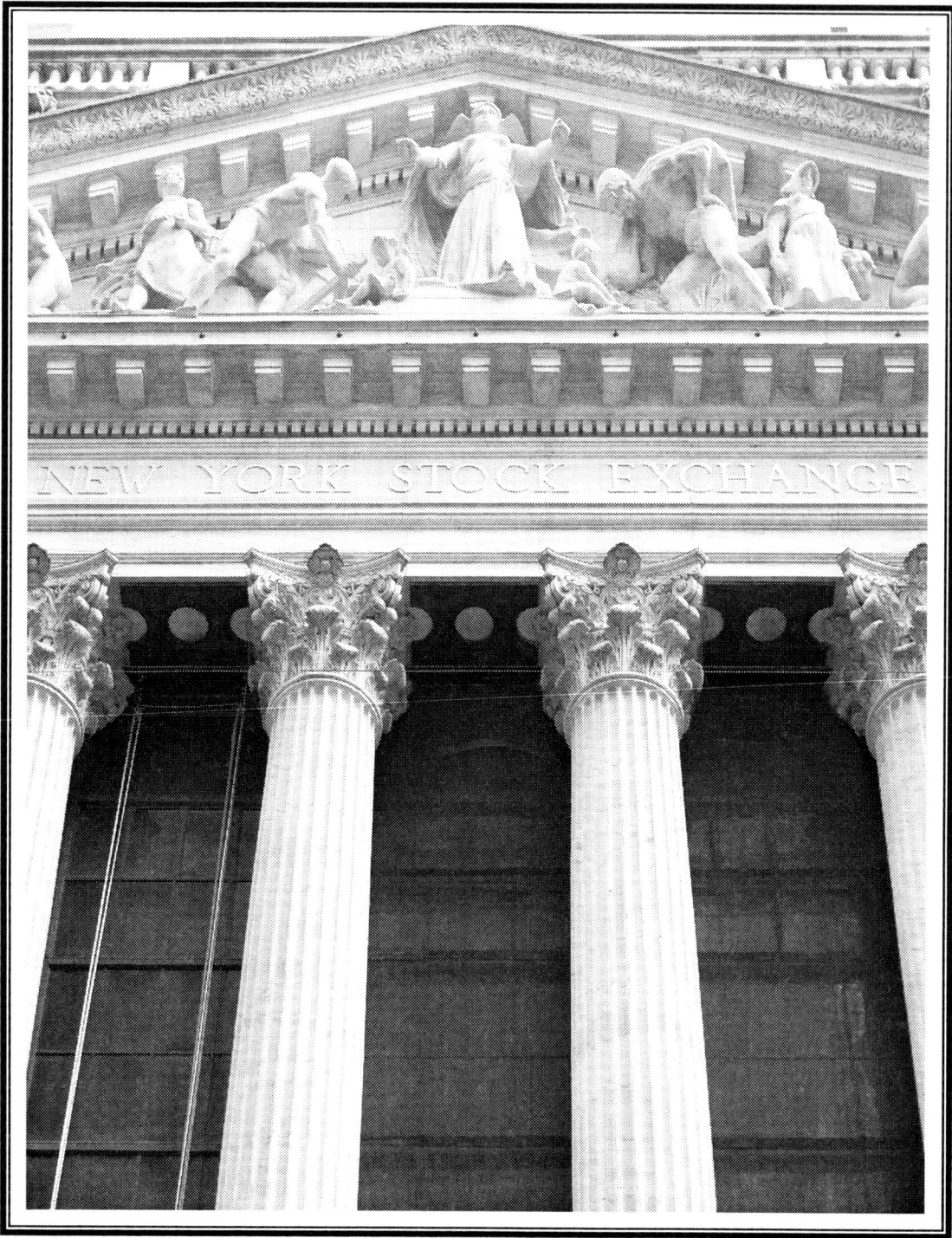

WHEN BANKS FOCUS ON CUSTOMERS, OUTSTANDING RESULTS FOLLOW: INSIGHTS FROM TWENTY YEARS OF STRATEGIC REDESIGN

Introduction

Oh, how times have changed. Since the original publication of this book in 2006, the banking industry and U.S. economy at large have undergone a dramatic downward spiral triggered by the sub-prime lending crisis. More than half a year into what many expect will officially be declared the start of a new growth cycle, and amid signs of strengthening momentum, the industry remains subdued about the prospects for further near-term improvement. This period of reconstruction presents bankers with a host of new challenges, as we tread cautiously in search of a return to normalcy.

Since 2008, nearly 240 U.S. banks and thrifts have failed in the wake of the financial crisis, combining for nearly $600 billion in assets and over $400 billion in deposits. After bottoming out in 2008, overall industry earnings have showed signs of recovery in certain segments, but remain threateningly low.

Bankers must overcome a range of obstacles to realize a positive outcome. The obstacles include their own caution — evident in credit standards that were repeatedly ratcheted up for more than two years — and what bankers characterized as weak demand and weak loan applicants.

As financial institutions face the challenges of the current economy, creativity is essential for our recovery. In particular, the vast capital destruction witnessed over the past three years, compounded by the pro-cyclical demand for incremental capital, would seem to demand new ideas; and potentially of greater importance, the resurgence of "old" ideas and the fundamental competitive tactics that remain relevant to the ever-changing dynamics of the banking industry.

Return on Average Assets (ROAA)
SNL Bank Index by Asset Segment 2005—2009

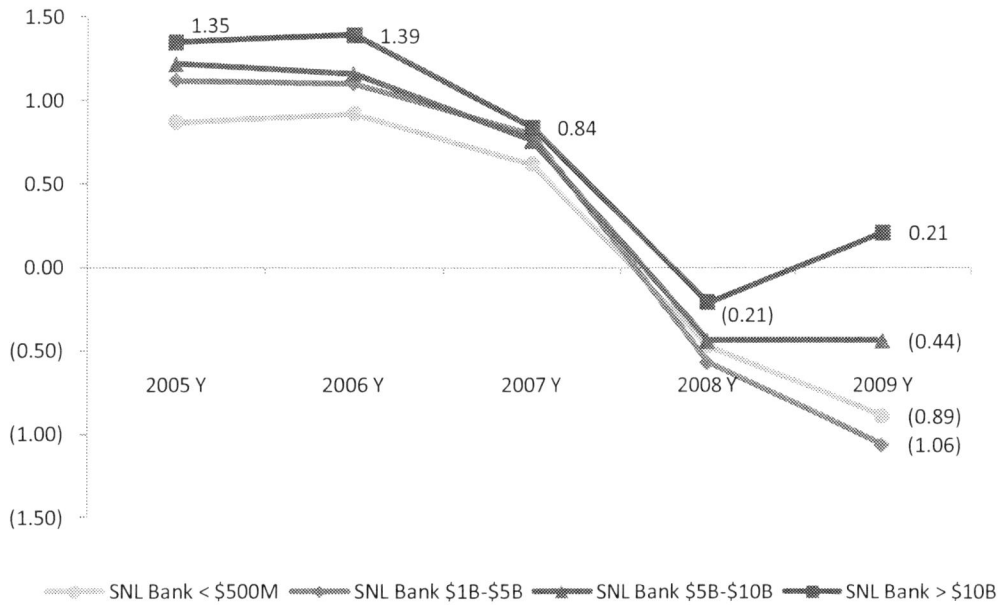

1.35
1.39
0.84
0.21
(0.21)
(0.44)
(0.89)
(1.06)

2005 Y   2006 Y   2007 Y   2008 Y   2009 Y

SNL Bank < $500M   SNL Bank $1B-$5B   SNL Bank $5B-$10B   SNL Bank > $10B

Failed Banks and Thrifts 2008 - 2010*
Dollars in Billions

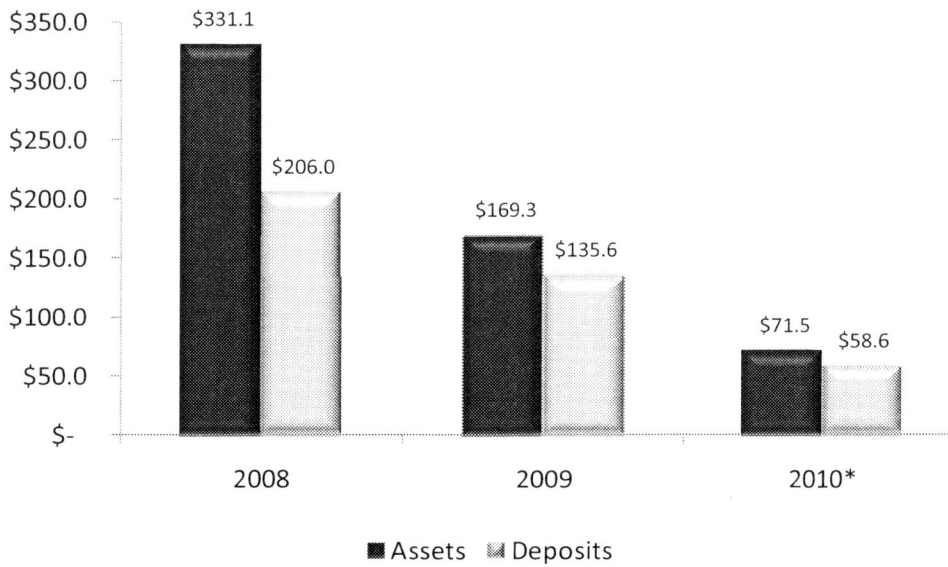

$331.1
$206.0
$169.3
$135.6
$71.5
$58.6

2008   2009   2010*

■ Assets ▦ Deposits

Source: SNL Financial   * 2010 data as of June, 2010

Over the past year, government-assisted deals have dominated the tame merger and acquisition market, and that trend will continue for the foreseeable future. However, unassisted deals should start to rebound in the second half of 2010 provided the economy improves and the uncertain regulatory environment and stock markets stabilize.

The rising number of failures has put the FDIC front and center in the bank-merger market. The agency is exerting more control over how deals are done – and who is doing them. Private equity is still interested, but is being forced to get creative to deal with restrictions the FDIC has imposed.

US Bank M&A Summary:
Bank and Thrift Whole Deals 2000 - 2009

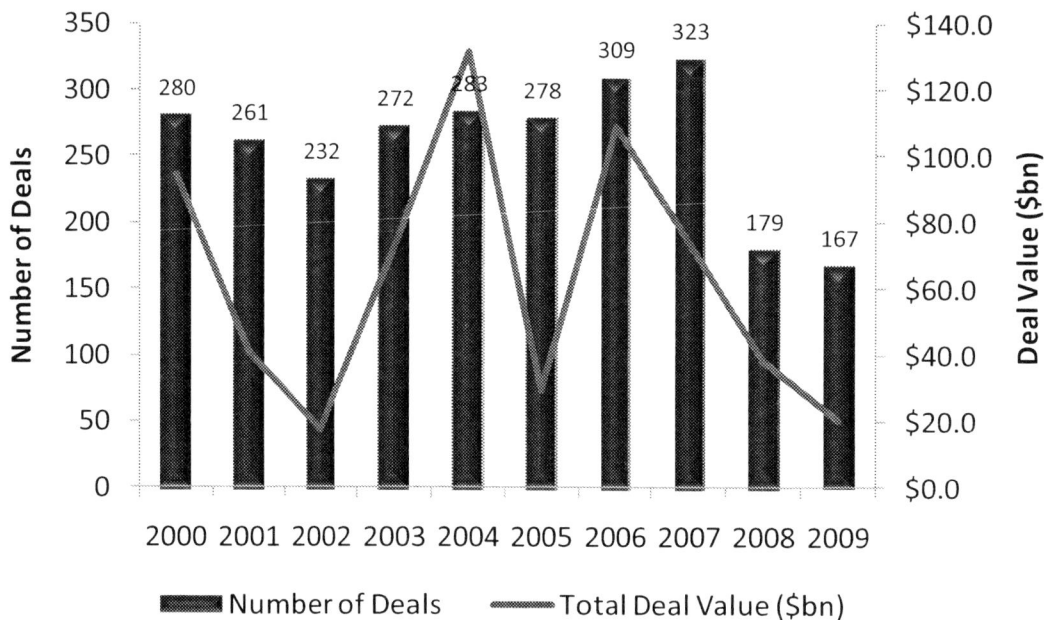

Bank failures are not expected to taper off before next year, nor do we expect the pace of FDIC-assisted deals to diminish significantly over coming months. But, as others in the industry have noted, assisted deals are becoming less financially appealing to some would-be buyers, particularly in the wake of changes to loss-sharing agreements. At the same time, some

Source: SNL Financial

potential buyers are growing increasingly strong, both in terms of excess capital and improving earnings.

Well Capitalized and Ready to Consolidate TCE / TA by Geographic Area 2009

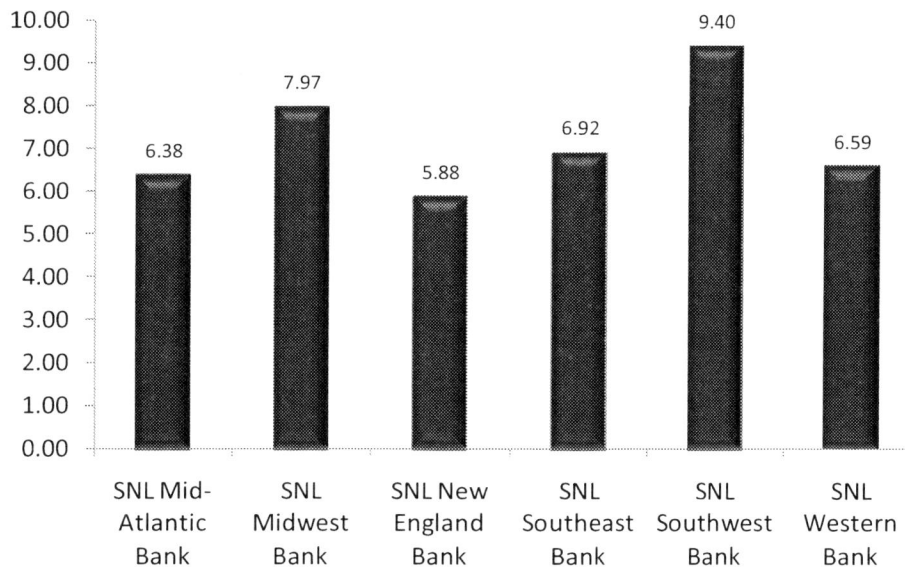

As these developments play out, healthy buyers may skip the FDIC-assisted process, especially as the field of targets gets increasingly picked over, and instead go after appealing open banks that, while sure to be survivors, might sell at a more favorable price this year or early next than they will a few years from now. We expect traditional deals to gather momentum only gradually over the next couple years as increasingly strong players pick off weaker competitors to gain market share.

Despite all of the speculation, what we do know to be true is that the banks who will emerge from the market environment and cycle of consolidation as being truly successful are those who create an integrated, long-term strategic M&A plan as opposed to those who choose to focus on individual transactions as they become available and elect to define strategy in an ad hoc fashion.

Source: SNL Financial

As I reflect on the future of the industry, it strikes me how now, more than ever, competitive edge will be found in exploring core strengths and distinctive strategies, as opposed to simply following the "the bank across the street."

Since 1990, nearly 48% or over 7,200 banks have disappeared from the map, and it is certainly anticipated that this rate will increase in the immediate term.

Total Number of Banks in the United States 1990 - 2010*

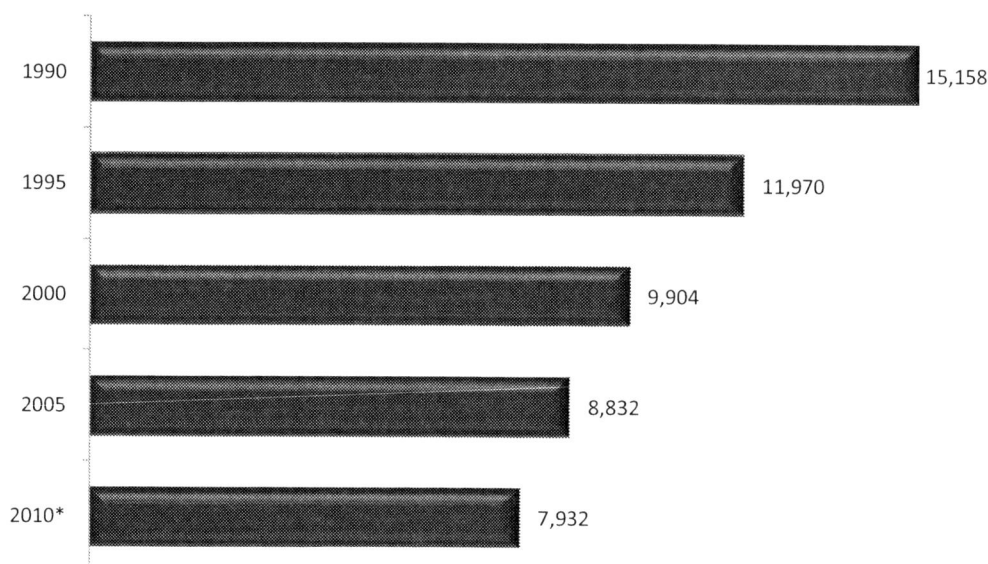

Year	Number
1990	15,158
1995	11,970
2000	9,904
2005	8,832
2010*	7,932

It is true that consolidation and better technology have resulted in a more efficient industry. The overall cost to income ratio for commercial banks is down to 57% in 2009, and overall operating expense has trended steadily downward as the industry has consolidated.

As the pending wave of consolidation continues over the next decade, banks will have to do more than simply rely on economies of scale to manage costs in order to compete effectively.

Source: FDIC   * 2010 data as of March 31, 2010

Efficiency Ratio (%) 1993 - 2009
SNL Bank Index

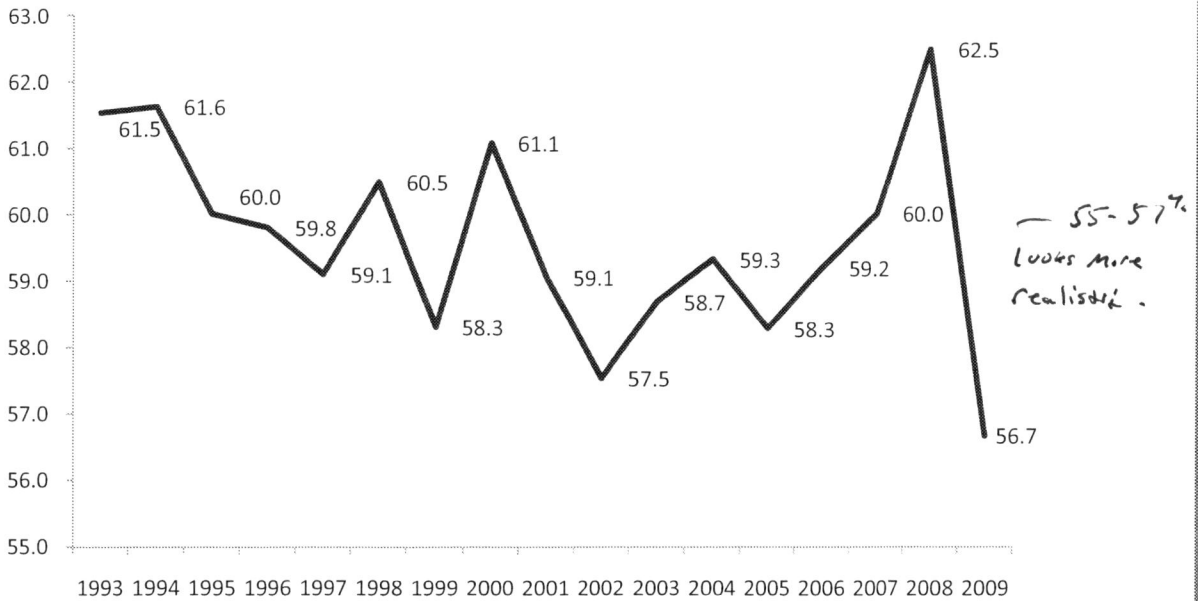

— 55-57%
looks more
realistic.

Operating Expense / Average Assets (%) 1993 - 2009
SNL Bank Index

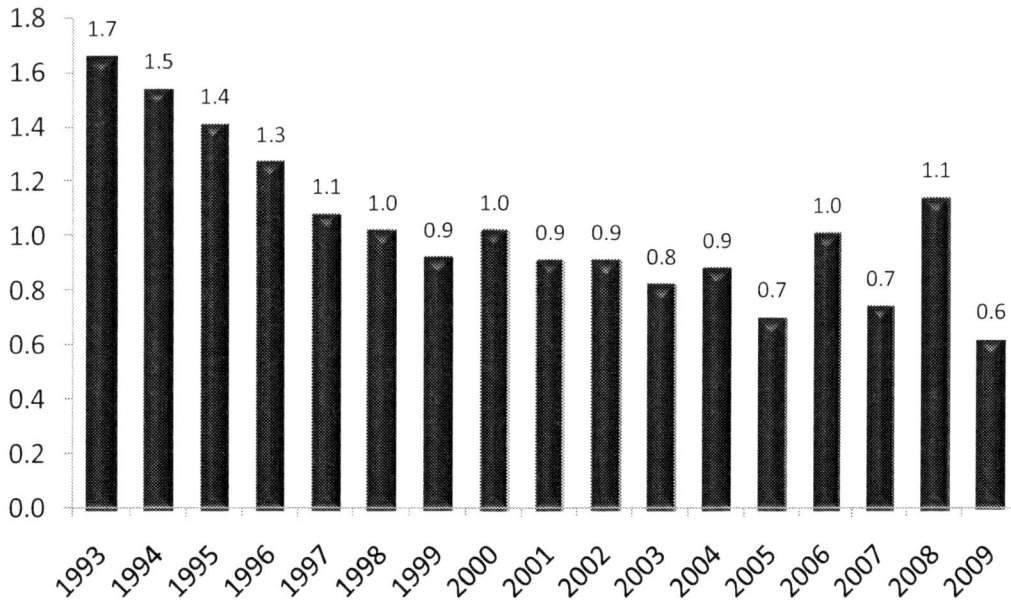

Source: SNL Financial

Despite the steady consolidation over the past 20 years, the banking industry in the US remains highly fragmented by international standards, as indicated by the share of assets accounted for by the top five banks as a percentage of all banks' assets.. There exists a significant concentration and effectiveness/efficiency gap between the US and other major markets.

Top 5 Banks Assets as a % of all Bank Assets 2009

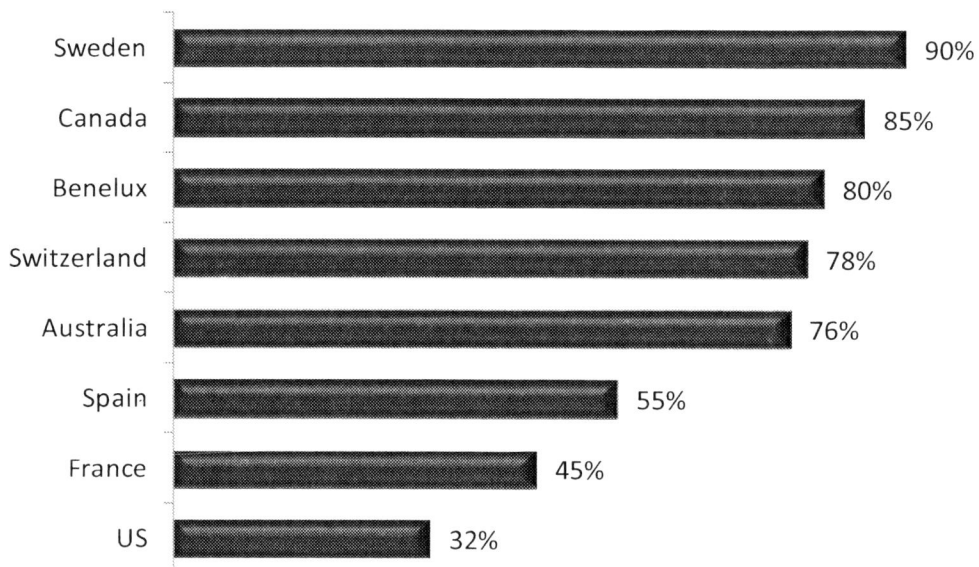

Country	%
Sweden	90%
Canada	85%
Benelux	80%
Switzerland	78%
Australia	76%
Spain	55%
France	45%
US	32%

Additional external factors and legislative action have created new pressures impacting both the top and bottom line.

Industry observers expect the changes to Regulation E, which will become mandatory in July 2010 and apply to ATM or one-time debit transactions by retail customers, to punch a hole in noninterest fee income that retail banks have come to depend on deeply in the wake of the subprime lending crisis and the investment crunch.

In order to compete and maintain earnings, banks will have to reassess fundamentally how they charge for perceived value, and get creative with supplementing their fee income lines.

Source: BIS Annual Report 2009

Non Interest Income / Operating Revenue (%)
1993 - 2009 SNL Bank and Thrift

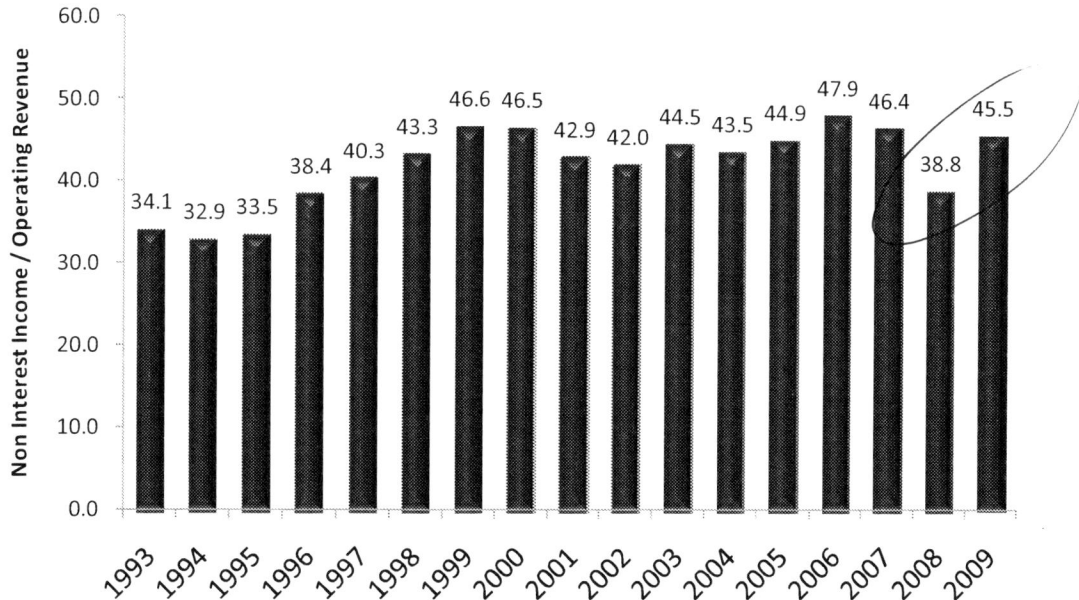

Non Interest Income / Operating Revenue

Year	Value
1993	34.1
1994	32.9
1995	33.5
1996	38.4
1997	40.3
1998	43.3
1999	46.6
2000	46.5
2001	42.9
2002	42.0
2003	44.5
2004	43.5
2005	44.9
2006	47.9
2007	46.4
2008	38.8
2009	45.5

After first publishing *"Reengineering the Bank"* in 1994, I mutually agreed with the many potential clients who appeared to be looking for quick "slash-and-burn cost-cutting" exercises that we could not help them. Rather, we have worked with those seeking fundamentally better ways to serve the customer. Our role in working with clients is summarized in our beliefs and aspirations:

- We do not aspire to define the client's strategy for them. The client works with us to set strategy, and translates it with us into distinct action drivers.

- As a result, each strategic design is unique. We are not "expert advisors" with the answer. Different strategic opportunities will require widely different approaches and result in distinctive outcomes.

Source: SNL Financial

- The crux of a successful strategic design is creating focus on real, measurable action across the organization to successfully attain major strategic goals.

- Design is about "doing better things," not "doing the same things at lower cost." The financial impact of strategic design should therefore be an outcome of, not input to, the design.

I am extremely proud of the impact we have had with our clients over the years. Of all their strengths, their ability systematically and continually to harvest employees' ideas and turn them into action is perhaps the one that I cherish the most. This is the one capability that we work in cooperation with senior management to instill in each of our clients.

Total Return (%) of Aston Clients v. SNL Bank Index
June 2000 - June 2010

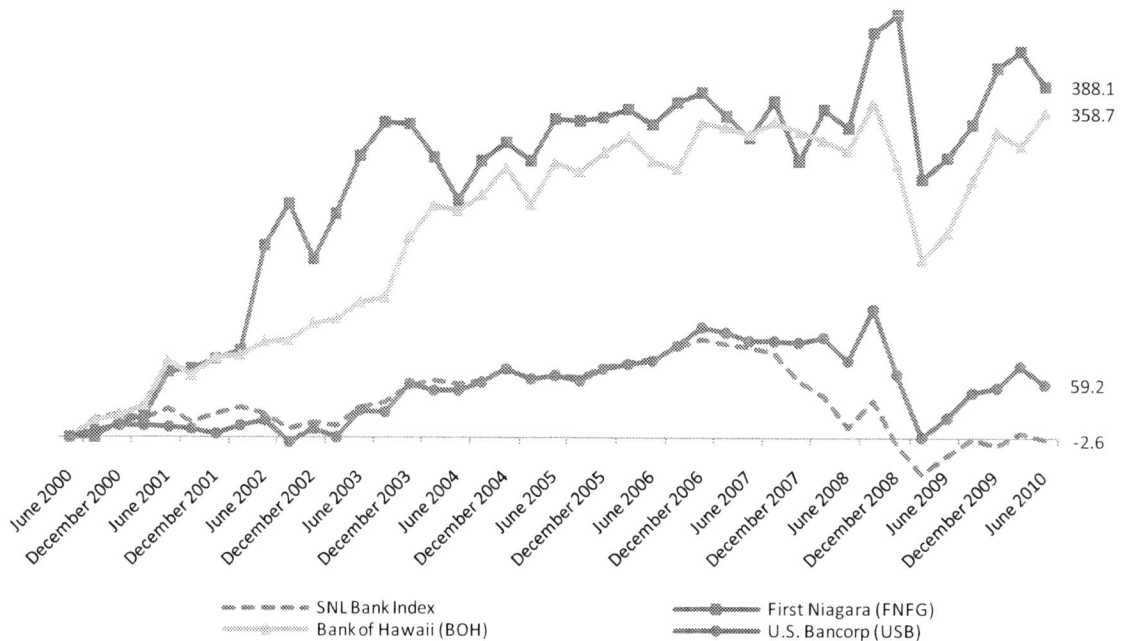

388.1
358.7
59.2
-2.6

SNL Bank Index
Bank of Hawaii (BOH)
First Niagara (FNFG)
U.S. Bancorp (USB)

In the following collection of articles, we present a plethora of insight for today's bank CEOs and for the 2.1 million or so bankers who are their colleagues. The collection is in some cases updated to reflect our latest thinking on a number of "hot topics." In other cases, the original work is presented, as the core ideas still carry tremendous impact. While the topics range widely, the observant reader will notice that our beliefs and aspirations are weaved like a red thread through every piece. This gives me confidence that we not only do as we say, but that our approach has withstood the test of time as we have carried the same message consistently and confidently for twenty years and more. We and our clients must be doing something right!

For those who want to continue thriving independently in the next twenty years, the following material helps in thinking how to do so. We will be there with you. Best of luck – and enjoy the ride!

With best regards,

Paul Allen

Chairman

Aston Associates

Princeton, New Jersey 2010

mutual fund
CREDIT CRUNCH
endorses stimulus package
Emergency loan
dollar
CAPITAL INVESTMENT
slow revival
Financial crisis
dollar weakens
STOCK MARKET
Inflation
earnings
analysts
Downturn
Profits down
slump
Confidence wobbles
Economic disaster looming
SHARES WORTHLES
Worldwide
Stocks tumble
assets
Crash!
anxiety deepens
Interest rates
survival in doubt
risk
RECESSION FORECAST
mortgage
key indice
MONETARY POLICY
Offshore
Bust!
Global trends

THE FINANCIAL CRISIS: PREDICTIVE INSIGHTS

Chapter 1 Introduction

Our first chapter begins with a discussion of some of the key industry key trends and tell-tail signs which we predicted both before and at the onset of the financial crisis.

As the number of failed banks and the FDIC list of troubled institutions continues to grow, private equity firms and investor groups have increasingly sought to get in on the action. Plenty of investor groups have knocked at the FDIC's door looking for the opportunity to buy failed banks, but only a handful of experienced teams have been successful. There is no question that private equity firms and investor groups looking to participate in government-assisted deals have to meet a higher standard than their strategic counterparts—and strategic buyers do have an advantage over private capital investors when bidding for failed banks, not only because the latter must adhere to more stringent requirements but also because strategic buyers can also include potential synergies from the deal in their bids.

As we continue to monitor how this combative relationship of potential suitors continues to play out, we start this book with the article "The Perfect Storm: Private Capital to the Rescue?," which we wrote at the start of the financial crisis—the conclusions of which have helped us greatly over the past eighteen months as we continue to examine the potential for true value creation through the infusion of private capital into the banking industry.

Our second piece in this chapter highlights some of the challenges that we predicted in 2005 for the mortgage industry entitled "Mortgage Industry May Face a Perfect Storm." The growth in the packaging and securitization of unconventional products and incredible spike in loan-to-value levels in the middle part of the decade resulted in the market correction which sent shock waves through the industry—the effects of which we continue to feel today. We did not know how right we would be!

NPA / Assets (%) 1993 - 2009
SNL Bank and Thrift Index

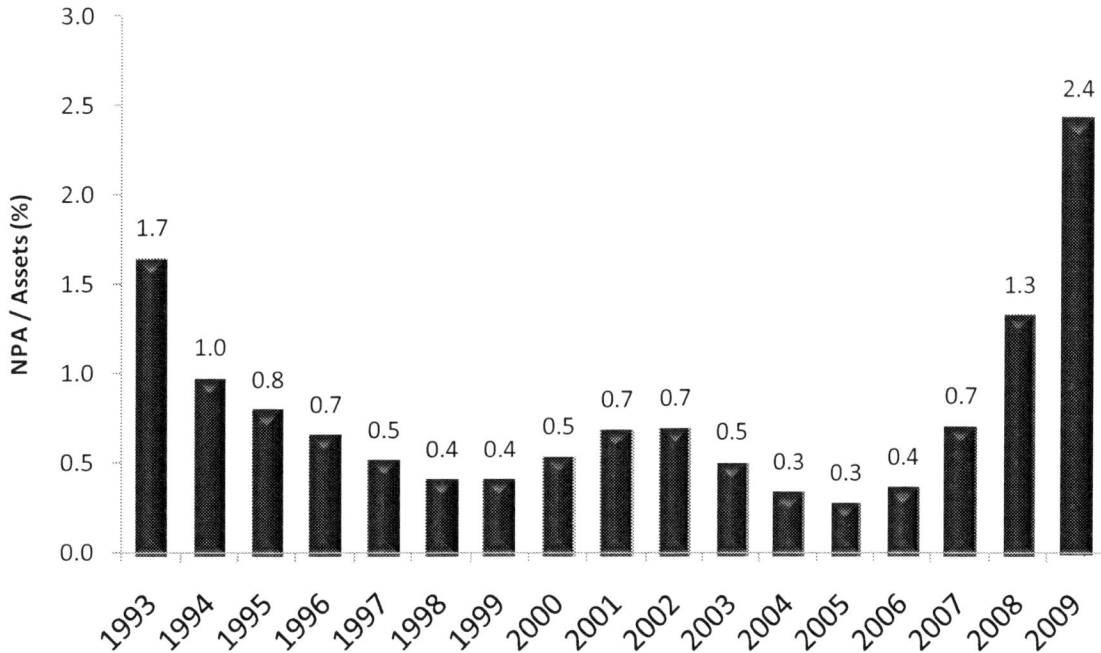

NPA / Assets (%)

Values: 1993: 1.7, 1994: 1.0, 1995: 0.8, 1996: 0.7, 1997: 0.5, 1998: 0.4, 1999: 0.4, 2000: 0.5, 2001: 0.7, 2002: 0.7, 2003: 0.5, 2004: 0.3, 2005: 0.3, 2006: 0.4, 2007: 0.7, 2008: 1.3, 2009: 2.4

Major Indices Price Change (%) June 2007—June 2010

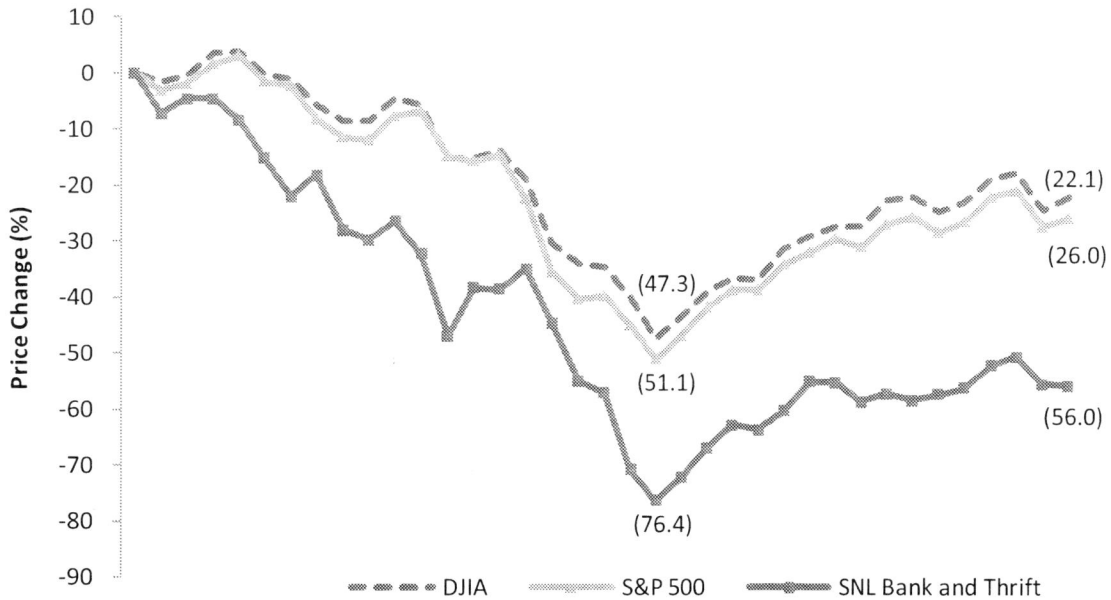

Price Change (%)

(47.3), (51.1), (76.4), (22.1), (26.0), (56.0)

Legend: DJIA, S&P 500, SNL Bank and Thrift

Source: SNL Financial

The Perfect Storm:
Private Capital to the Rescue?

Article originally published in American Banker on September 24, 2008

Reprinted with permission

When we wrote Reengineering The Bank in 1994 at the nadir of the last major credit crunch, we said large banks "could use their superior credit underwriting skills to embrace the new technology of securitization and other structured finance to establish a defensible role" in wholesale credit markets. We added that community and regional banks could learn from the past underwriting failures in commercial real estate lending and loan participations (funding LBO financing and other excesses) that caused the write-off debacle of $108 billion between 1990-1992.

It's hard to believe it's déjà vu all over again. The market capitalization of twenty-nine of the largest financial firms in the US has declined 47% from $1.86 trillion at the market high on October 9, 2007, to $0.98 trillion on September 12, 2008. Six of these firms (Bear Sterns, Lehman Bros, Fannie, Freddie, AIG and Merrill Lynch) are nationalized, absorbed or bankrupt at a cost to shareholders, at last count, of $376 billion. Others, like Washington Mutual and Morgan Stanley, perhaps stand at the brink.

Meanwhile, many regional and community banks are struggling with investment security devaluations and residential and commercial real estate cesspools. For banks with total assets under $50 billion, second quarter net charge offs increased 136% from $5.5 billion in Q207 to $13.1 billion in Q208. Their non-current loans to loans ratio increased from 0.9% to 2.0%. Their loan loss allowance to non-current loans fell from 122% to 72%.

The sources of such calamity? For many large commercial banks, it was an abdication of underwriting standards and accountability as they trusted investment bankers to be able, by slight of hand, to turn appallingly weak credit into high quality securities through pooling, tranching and credit enhancement; to understand credit risk better than they did. For many smaller commercial banks, it was a herd mentality of seeking easy, burgeoning earnings through a credit binge of real estate driven balance sheet growth based on exotic product design (such as pay-option ARMs and negative-amortization loans) that bore no signs of prudent underwriting. And for both groups there was simple greed. Added to all of this was woeful oversight by examiners and rating agencies.

We warned in the "American Banker" of December 30, 2005 that with, "housing prices plummeting; overcapacity causing irrational pricing; credit losses mounting... there is the risk of a 'perfect storm' over the next stage of the business/interest rate cycle". Unfortunately, the financial markets' equivalent of Katrina has indeed hit.

There are exceptions. Past bank partners of Aston Associates, whether large, like US Bancorp, regionally dominant, like Bank of Hawaii, or emerging super community, like First Niagara, maintained rigorous credit standards; followed a clear strategic direction; focused on core operating effectiveness; invested only in securities they understood; and are thriving. All are actually trading near or above their stock price at the October 9, 2007 market top. Moreover, the US financial system will weather the storm, provided the Treasury and the Federal Reserve stop reacting and proactively help lead investors from the psychological brink of panic.

Yet, to quote an excellent article in American Banker by Joseph Rizzi of CapGen Financial Group, "The downsizing and recapitalization efforts at many institutions are remedies, not strategies. Capital alone is insufficient, as evidenced by the continued stock declines after record capital increases. Investors require new strategies to generate revenue to offset the declining structured finance business at large institutions and the C&D declines at community banks. These discredited business models had generated the majority of income growth at these institutions." Given that discredited models and financial leverage drove earnings at many banks, their decline will create excess capacity and will decimate short-term returns and dividend payouts. The current $150 billion capital influx (with many multiples of that to come) feeds the paradox of refunding undercapitalized institutions in an industry that is overcapitalized relative to sustainable business opportunities. Let the investor beware who throws money at this situation without clarity on longer- term sources of value. The recent providers of $65 billion of capital have already experienced major losses, including the $21 billion in equity capital raised by Merrill Lynch in 2008 before its shotgun wedding to Bank of America.

However, private equity firms and hedge funds can smell opportunity in the current debacle and are putting pressure on regulators to let them get in the game. Currently, the Fed subjects principal investors to greater oversight if they exceed a 9.9% voting stake in a bank, when they may be deemed to have a "controlling interest" and to be a bank holding company, triggering restrictions on non-banking activities and leverage. To avoid these consequences, investors can agree to be passive, but that puts limits on their board representation and operating management oversight. The Federal Reserve is weighing three measures to spur private investment. One measure would allow firms to use silo funds to buy banks, which would protect their core fund from bank holding company regulation. Another would let private equity firms exercise more control of banks in which they have invested. And the third would encourage private investors to team up on bank deals. Additionally, the Fed is considering allowing funds to amass up to a third of a bank in a mixture of voting and nonvoting stock while also taking more active oversight roles and filling board seats. All of these measures are intended to aid in the deployment of large amounts of idle capital.

Indeed, investment activity is already intense with TPG Inc leading a group that injected $7 billion into Washington Mutual in April; Corsair Capital leading investors to pump $7 billion into National City; the Carlyle Group taking a $75 million stake in Boston Private Financial Holdings which owns five banks; CIVC Partners investing $50 million in Wintrust Financial; and MattlinPatterson Global Advisors rescuing Thornburg Mortgage and reportedly looking closely at BankUnited and Downey Financial. However, from the public announcements on some of these deals, we cannot see where the value will be created that either justifies the premia paid or is implicit in the conversion ratios.

To date, the current situation has differed from the savings and loan crisis of the 1980s and 1990s when 747 S&L associations failed and $294 billion was lost. During that crisis US taxpayers absorbed most of the loss and thereby created huge value for acquiring banks and investors who were given cheap deposits and infrastructure while having recourse for bad credits through the Resolution Trust Corporation.

The Federal Reserve desperately tried to avoid taking this approach to dealing with the crisis we now face. Examiners put the squeeze on nearly every bank we know to increase their capital ratios by curtailing lending to shrink their risk asset base and by raising funds through private placements and capital market forays. The hope was that private investors would fund the workout rather than taxpayers. The fact that this may increase capital unnecessarily in fundamentally sound institutions, exacerbating the credit crunch; and may throw good money after bad in fundamentally unsound ones is moot – the regulators will have their way. However, ultimately, it may well be that the Treasury and the Fed are forced into a solution similar to the RTC model, perhaps at a cost over $1 trillion. In either event, there will be opportunities for "vulture funds" to acquire failed institutions and to bottom-fish distressed assets from sound institutions who sell them below value simply to get them off their books. This play depends primarily upon the investor being able to both assess the true default loss exposure through exceptional due diligence and to work out the credit problems better than the disposing institution.

However, the true opportunity for sustained returns from long-term investments in sound financial institutions facing immediate capital needs comes from identifying real strategic and operating potential. In an industry with sudden and increasing excess supply and diminishing speculative demand, success in the foreseeable future will be driven by gaining market share from competitors and achieving operating (not financial) leverage from each dollar of business won. A player operating at the industry average of 61 cents of cost for every dollar of revenue will not win against one operating at 48 cents of cost. The savvy investor will look to invest in banks with operating models based on pragmatic, sustainable performance advantages executed effectively (not simply efficiently). Investors will then be faced with the imperative of marshaling resources that can capitalize on these advantages through exceptional due diligence, deal structuring and operational management. A challenge that is far more difficult than many inexperienced investors understand.

There is incredible potential for value creation in an environment where the Federal Reserve encourages private equity investment in banks (rather than sets up the roadblocks of past regulation). However, there is also the risk of being an optimistic investor faced with a black hole of credit risk exposure that can absorb capital injections like raindrops into a lake.

Mortgage Industry May Face a "Perfect Storm"

Article originally published in American Banker on
December 30, 2005

Reprinted with permission

Mortgage companies have been richly rewarded in recent years. Originations have grown a staggering 16% a year, on average, since 1990; excluding refinancing the figure is a solid 9%. Still, originations have been down in six of those years, largely because of refinance volume. Mortgage production peaked in 2003 at $3.8 trillion, driven by $2.5 trillion of refinancing. It has slipped since then, though this year the total is estimated to be the third-highest ever.

Fueled by refinancing and continued strength in housing markets, the industry has added significant capacity in recent years. Consolidation and the resulting economies of scale have also contributed to profitability; from 1990 to 2003 the top 10 originators went from 17% of the market to 61%, and the top 25 went from 28% to 77%.

Topping off the tide of good fortune has been record-low charge-offs, which reflect low interest rates, sound economic growth, and ever-rising home prices. At thrifts, for example, troubled assets have steadily declined, from 3.8% in 1990 to 0.34% in this year's second quarter.

But the next three to five years could prove difficult. To date in 2005, the S&P thrift and mortgage finance index is down about 15%, reflecting reduced production and investor wariness about four issues; which could, together, create a catastrophic scenario.

A real estate slump. In a September report the Fed staff argued that housing is less overvalued than traditional measures like price/rent and price/income ratios suggest. More sophisticated ratios using imputed rents show prices to be reasonable, they claimed. But last year, Yale economist Robert Shiller told the Fed that housing prices in major cities showed several characteristics of a bubble. Moreover, mortgage banks had failed to use hedging techniques that would enable them to withstand a prolonged downturn in the housing market, he contended.

September's 20% increase in homes available for sale, along with the highest inventory of new homes since 1996 could mean Prof. Shiller was right. Forecasters at the Mortgage Bankers Association predict a 19% tumble in originations next year as refinancings sag while housing starts and sales of existing homes drop 3.5%.

Should a serious correction occur, demand for home equity products would fall and mortgage producers would be more cautious in offering "exotic" and higher-risk products — for example, pay-option ARMs and interest-only loans.

Given the growth in unconventional products recently and current loan-to-value levels — balances of loans for 90% or more of value totaled almost $25 billion in 2005, 88% more than in June 2004 — a correction could send shock waves through the industry. In Hong Kong, for example, a plunge in property prices sent the aggregate LTV to 121% in 2003, despite a guideline limiting the ratio in property lending to 70%.

Funding costs. The industry also faces higher costs for traditional deposit gathering. In addition to having to pay higher rates, in the past few years lenders have made unprecedented investments in building branches.

Meanwhile technology, competitive capacity, and product innovation have put pressure on sources of non-interest and net interest income, as exemplified by the now industry-standard "free checking."

The combination of higher expenses and lower deposit fees and yields will keep adding pressure on earnings.

Overcapacity. The MBA estimates that next year refinance volume will fall more than 60% below the 2003 peak. Though some capacity is variable or could be redeployed, instant adjustment to plunging demand is unlikely. And overcapacity would surely put pressure on price and margin.

Credit losses. Finally, it is reasonable to expect that credit losses will trend back toward historic averages. Record-low rates and healthy economic growth helped chop the foreclosure rate to 0.06% of assets. In contrast, the historic rate (from 1967) was nine times higher, at 0.54%. With short-term rates already rising, these conditions are likely to normalize.

Housing prices plummeting. Funding costs skyrocketing. Overcapacity causing irrational pricing. Credit losses mounting.

Even if one or two of these things happen, the mortgage industry surely has challenging years ahead. The best that mortgage banks can do right now is prepare for a range of scenarios.

Top management has to involve all business units in identifying gaps in the current operating model. Such a discussion could address the operating and performance gaps that might arise from the expected 39% reduction in refinance volume next year.

The second step requires broad employee involvement and continued top-management guidance. Action programs need to be clearly defined; the risks and stakeholder impact must be assessed. For example, one mortgage originator wanted to capitalize on the increased value of existing servicing rights in a rising rate environment. Evaluating changes in its practice of selling new production instead of holding loans in portfolio enabled it to put a clear plan in place.

Next, the executive team needs to meet to set priorities so it can implement a plan, usually in 12 to 18 months. For example, to position itself for a changing environment one regional mortgage bank made it a priority to refine its products for builders of single-family and multifamily homes.

Finally, though accountability for implementation should be distributed across the organization, it is a good idea for a dedicated implementation team to track it. And, we have found that the tracking tools and resources can pay for themselves many times over.

*   *   *

The mortgage banking industry has shown itself to be robust in dealing with past downturns. However, there is a risk of the "perfect storm" over the next stage of the business/interest rate cycle. Now is the time to proactively prepare for the worst; and so better ride out whatever magnitude of downturn we face.

Chapter Two

RESHAPING AN INDUSTRY THROUGH MERGERS & ACQUISITIONS

Chapter 2 Introduction

Our journey continues in the arena of mergers and acquisitions. During our years of helping bankers to out-perform competition, we have been part of many successful mergers and integrations, and observed even more botched deals.

The tumultuous industry conditions and troubled financial markets of the past two years has spawned an unprecedented deal environment filled with everything from government assisted deals and loss-sharing arrangements to creative carve-outs. Notwithstanding the recent drop off in open-bank M&A resulting from the crisis, mergers and acquisitions will continue (and likely accelerate) in banking for the foreseeable future, and despite a steady stream of consolidation throughout our careers, the industry remains highly fragmented, and synergy opportunities abound.

It is therefore appropriate to start this chapter with an article titled "What Does and Doesn't Matter in M&A Strategy," which examines three myths that exist in banking around bank size, revenue growth and performance. We were inspired to write this piece when a bank CEO told us that in his opinion you have to choose either a "growth" or a "performance" path, but not both. (We disagreed).

The next two articles "To Sell or Not to Sell? Here's How to Decide" and "In Busy M&A Generation, Few Deals Brought Value Promised," both advise Board of Directors and CEOs on how to avoid the classic traps of bad deals (or, at least, good deals badly integrated).

Who will acquire and who will be acquired in the future? Only time can tell, but learning from experience is not a bad place to start.

Total Number of Banking M&A Deals in the United States
1990-2009

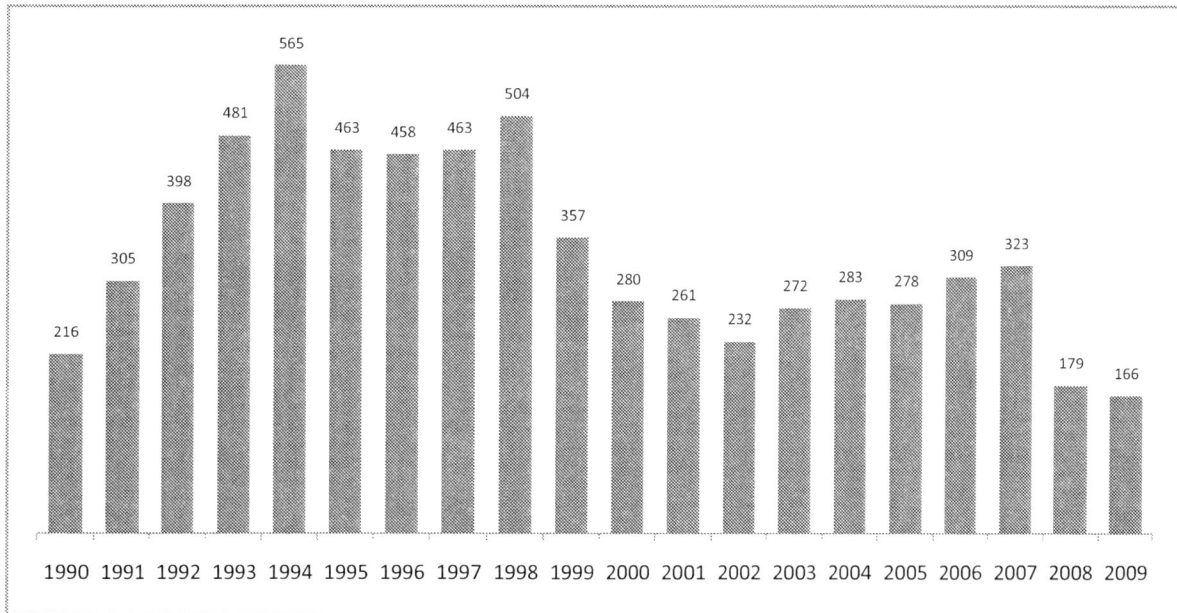

Year	Value
1990	216
1991	305
1992	398
1993	481
1994	565
1995	463
1996	458
1997	463
1998	504
1999	357
2000	280
2001	261
2002	232
2003	272
2004	283
2005	278
2006	309
2007	323
2008	179
2009	166

Total Number of Banks in the United States 1990-2010*

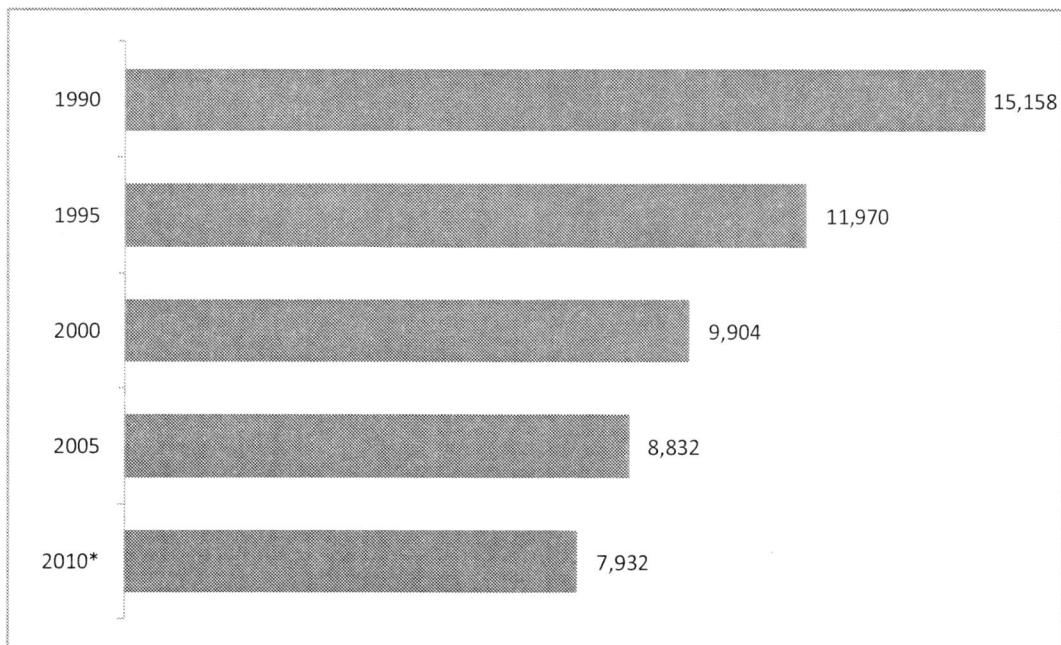

Year	Value
1990	15,158
1995	11,970
2000	9,904
2005	8,832
2010*	7,932

Source: FDIC   * 2010 data as of March 31

What Does and Doesn't Matter in M&A Strategy

Article originally published in American Banker on April 15, 2005

Reprinted with permission

What is the optimal size for a U.S. bank in 2005? Is there a natural break-point, where cost and revenue efficiencies and economies of scale become dominated by diseconomies of scale and scope? If not, our country's largest banking companies should be the best performers. In reality, examining *American Banker*'s "top 150" lists of 2004 on the performance measures of return on equity, return on assets and efficiency ratio, shows a very different picture: of the 25 largest banking companies, four make the top 25 ROE and ROA lists, and only one makes the top 25 efficiency ratio list.

Mega-mergers like BoA/Fleet and JPM/BankOne are leading the way in forming new trillion-dollar asset entities, and M&A activity and pricing have become increasingly heated throughout the industry. A "more is better" philosophy appears solidly ingrained as acquisitions are announced, touting expense synergies of up to 30% of the target's operating expenses in order to justify high acquisition premiums. The logical inference from this "size race" is that banks that grow rapidly through acquisition achieve better financial performance.

However, in our recent review of the top 150 U.S. banks with assets above $4 billion, we found no positive correlation between financial performance and size, or between financial performance and rate of growth. Based on this, banks that aim to deliver top performance going forward should consider a sober, disciplined approach to M&A in a broader strategic context. Where this exists, acquisitions can accelerate strategic success; where not, they can exacerbate ineffectiveness.

Myth #1: Bigger is better: Among the 150 largest U.S. based banks (by asset size), we found no significant correlation (positive or negative) between size and performance indicators (ROA, ROE and efficiency ratio). The average compound annual growth in the sample was 15% (from 1999 to 2003), ROA was 1.3%, ROE 15.4% and efficiency ratio 56%.

Traditionally, industry and academic research has argued that scale and scope economies are most relevant in the mergers of smaller banks. Through the mid-1990s, it was generally accepted that scale efficiencies were exhausted somewhere in the asset size range of between $2 and $10 billion (Berger and Humphrey of the Federal Reserve, 1994). In their 1997 study of bank efficiencies using 1990s data, Berger and Mester found that scale benefits were achieved up to $25 billion in assets. They attributed this change during the 1990s to larger banks being better able to leverage: reduction in open-market interest rates; removal of regulatory restrictions associated with bank branching and holding company expansion; and improvements in technology (e.g., ATM networks, credit scoring) and applied finance (e.g., derivative contracts and off-balance-sheet activities).

Potentially offsetting the factors identified by Berger and Mester and the relative advantage of mid-scale institutions is the access to increasingly sophisticated technologies for smaller banks. More vanilla solutions have become available to all sizes of players. Sophisticated, proprietary CRM tools and customer data warehouse solutions are no longer the domain of larger institutions only.

In our examination of the top 150 banks, we did not find any significant difference in financial performance between banks over and under $25 billion. On the contrary, we found high-growth, high performance organizations at both ends of the size scale. With $190 billion in assets, U.S. Bancorp tops the size, growth and performance charts with 20% annual growth from 1992 to 2004, 22% ROE, 2.1% ROA and 44% efficiency ratio. Their dedication to a strategy of customer service has proven itself over more than a decade of spectacular performance. Similarly, towards the bottom of the size chart, with $5 billion in assets, Pacific Capital Bancorp outperformed its peers on all measures: 28% ROE, 2.1% ROA and 47% efficiency ratio. Both banks have approximately doubled their share price in the last five years, delivering returns to shareholders more than twice the overall bank index.

Myth #2: Smaller is better: Industry observers have questioned the value to shareholders of the largest mergers. When Bank of America announced their acquisition of Fleet in October 2003, their stock price plunged almost 10% in the month following the announcement. However, *American Banker's* recent headline on reporting Bank of America's 2004 full year earnings was: "An 'I told you so' moment for CEO Lewis." With return on equity during 4Q 2004 already at 16%, efficiency ratio at 51% and return on assets at 1.4%, Bank of America is demonstrating that with effective customer integration, bigger can be good.

This is contrary to much common belief. The consensus view has traditionally been that the average cost curve in banking has a relatively flat U-shape, and that the largest banks have in fact a slight cost disadvantage to most of their smaller peers. There is, however, limited research (using relatively small sample sizes), to substantiate this. In our sample, we found no indication that the largest banks are at a disadvantage to their mid-size peers with respect to financial performance.

One reason the U-shape may no longer necessarily exist at the top end of the scale is that effective players can use scale to flex buying power effectively with suppliers. By utilizing reverse auctions, online bidding, automated and coordinated procurement, much of the waste that traditionally took place in larger banks, can potentially be reduced dramatically. Moreover, there are true scale effects of national branding, merchandising, marketing and promotion.

Myth #3: Growth and operating effectiveness are conflicting objectives. We also found no correlation between the rate of asset growth and performance indicators (ROA, ROE and efficiency ratio). A widely held belief among many bank executives is that you have to choose a strategy of either "growth" or "operating effectiveness." Our findings did not support this view.

Among the 150 largest banks, 21 had compound annual asset growth in excess of 25%. Their performance indicators in terms of ROA, ROE and efficiency ratio were no different from the overall sample. There are examples of less efficient, high growth companies such as Commerce Bancorp with 66% efficiency ratio and 36% annual growth. Conversely, companies like U.S. Bancorp have achieved similar growth levels over a longer time period and have demonstrated financial performance and an efficiency ratio that make their peers pale by comparison.

Similarly, at the other end of the scale, among the banking companies that actually contracted in size during the time period, there is a full spectrum of performance. There are examples of bottom-decile performers like UMB Financial Corporation, with compound annual asset growth of -1.2%, ROA of 0.5%, ROE of 6% and efficiency ratio of 85%. However, there are also top performers like Bank of Hawaii, which, by shrinking global scope to focus on its core markets, has reduced assets by more than 10% annually since 1999, and yet delivered ROE of 22% and ROA of 1.7%.

***

So what distinguishes the banks that consistently achieve growth and performance from those that do not, if size and growth rate are not per se primary drivers? In our experience, the four key distinguishing components are unrelenting focus on 1) strategy, 2) execution, 3) customers' needs, and 4) measurement and tracking. Regional banks that are in the $5-$15 billion range today and are looking to become $25 billion institutions in the future, should first and foremost to their strategic drivers.

Stick to your strategy: While financial performance reality indicates no link between performance and acquisitions, this does not mean that there is an inherent conflict between the two.

The former Signet Corporation created Capital One as an integral part of its growth strategy. Recognizing that it could not realize its vision for information-based consumer credit growth within the constraints of the existing company, Signet gave Richard Fairbank and Nigel Morris the go-ahead to drive Capital One as a separate entity. In the following decade, Capital One grew to $20 billion in market cap and delivered annual shareholder returns of staggering 34%. In absolute terms, a dollar invested in Capital One ten years ago is worth more than eighteen dollars today.

Focus on execution: Obviously, even the best planned strategy will fail if not executed well. Senior management team vision and charisma can only carry a banking franchise so far as it grows. At some point, process and structure must drive the vision across the organization. Simply relying on personality does not do it. With increasing size, diseconomies of scope are real, but they can be managed through exquisite execution.

Ambiguity is the best defense for status quo proponents and the worst enemy for change agents. Ill-defined and non-specific strategic programs rarely achieve much.

Research by Berger and Humphrey suggests that the average performing bank will have 20% higher costs than the "best in class" performer with same scale and scope. By quantifying expectations, specifying time lines and obsessing with tracking results, true strategic impact can be achieved. Action programs must be specific: What is expected when, by whom, and at what cost and benefit? While this may sound "apple pie," how many organizations truly specify and track that well?

Focus on the Customer: Whether a "grow and perform", or simply "perform" strategy is employed, the key to success is focus on the customer. Increasingly sophisticated tools for managing overall customer relationships are no longer available only to the largest players, but can be accessed by all banks on the top 150 list. Staying close to changes in customer behavior and monitoring and countering any developments in customer attrition is critical. Well-designed strategies should see significant improvements in retention of the most valuable customers. St. George Bank in Australia, a US$75 billion company that competes daily with four behemoth banks of over US$150 billion, has proven this point. By dramatically deepening its customer relationships, St. George Bank has achieved 20%+ annual revenue growth for more than five years without any significant acquisitions; and stock price appreciation of 22% a year, and now boasts more than seven products per customer among key customer segments. St. George was most recently recognized as the best bank in Australia by Money Magazine. Similarly, Wells Fargo focuses intensely on their relationship accounts and boasts eight products per customer in these important segments.

Establishing effective measurements and tracking: The design of tools for effectively measuring strategic impact is critical. Measures like customer and employee satisfaction, process change achievement and financial impact, which fit the specific objectives and needs of the organization, should be developed. The most effective banking companies referenced in this article have all established a rigorous set of key performance indicators in a weekly or monthly performance evaluation. In addition to financial measures, robust tracking of core customer segments, in terms of share of wallet and channel usage; production and sales success across organizational barriers; and in-depth customer attrition data, are key success indicators. As always, what gets measured gets done.

***

The banking myths "bigger is better," "smaller is better," and "choose growth or performance" are just that — myths. By driving a focused strategy, banks of very different sizes and growth rates may effectively achieve better growth and performance, and generate superior shareholder returns. No matter what M&A path is ultimately pursued, a disciplined, structured approach will leave senior executives and their board of directors with broader and better options for delivering future shareholder value.

To Sell of Not to Sell? Here's
How to Decide

Article originally published in American Banker on
February 4, 2005

Reprinted with permission

"Should I stay or should I go" may be the lyrics of an 80's pop song, but more importantly, for Board members of many regional banks today, it translates into a key question: is it in our shareholders' best interest to keep faith with our operating model and management team, or are we better off selling the bank? Given today's scrutiny on Board independence by regulators and shareholder activists, it is critical that Boards take a strategic and well-thought out approach to determining which path to take.

In 2004, the market for bank mergers and acquisitions continued to heat up. A total of 177 bank acquisitions took place through the 3rd quarter of 2004. Household names like BankOne, Charter One, Fleet, Provident (Ohio), Southtrust and Union Planters ceased to exist as independent entities last year. In fact, over the last three years, a total of 617 banks have been merged or acquired. Despite this activity of consolidation, the United States remains a fragmented market place, with a total of 8,032 FDIC-insured banks and savings institutions operating. Of total assets in FDIC insured institutions, still only 41% is controlled by the top five banks, while 64% is controlled by the twenty largest banks. Compare this to Canada, where 85% of assets are controlled by the top six banks, or

Australia, where 76% of assets are controlled by the top five banks. It is a safe bet to assume that consolidation will continue.

However, the value created for shareholders through consolidation remains unconvincing. Recent studies include a 1998 review by Federal Reserve members Steven Pilloff and Anthony Santomero and a 1999 update on banking mergers by Federal Reserve members Simon Kwan and Robert Eisenbeis. The latter found that more than half of the performance variables studied declined postmerger: there was a shift from positive to negative in the mean ROE based on operating income in the eight quarters that followed the merger; and the mean efficiency ratio post-merger fell by a marginal 0.34%.

While the majority of bank mergers may have failed to create value, there are powerful exceptions. U.S. Bancorp, under the leadership of Jerry Grundhofer, has grown from $7 billion of assets in 1992 to $209 billion today. During the course of this transformation, efficiency ratio has improved from 62% to 44% and the compound annual return to shareholders from 1992 to 2004 is a stellar 24%.

While rejecting a "just say no" strategy might have been an easy decision in the past, the picture is now more complex. Mirroring the overall M&A momentum, deal premiums have become increasingly rich in 2004, topping 2% completed price to equity for the first time since 1999. (At 2.17% in 2004, the completed price to equity has jumped significantly from 1.84% and 1.89% in 2002 and 2003, respectively.) Saying no to such returns may leave you open to question by the shareholders you represent.

When assessing whether a course of continued independence is warranted, directors of regional banks, particularly medium and smaller institutions, manage their own fate. Several factors should be considered. First, Boards need to assess the marketplace: local market conditions, changes in customer and business demographics, and the relative strength of competitors in the footprint. Secondly, the Board should consider their people in terms of leadership capability, management transition issues and overall bench strength. Thirdly, directors need to bear in mind community considerations, for example, erosion of community opportunities and jobs when closing an administrative center. Finally, macro-changes driven by the business cycle as well as interest rate and investment environment, will clearly impact the timing and attractiveness of a potential offer. But, most critical is whether the strategic operating model and executional capability of management justify independence.

In evaluating strategic options, there is no substitute for a disciplined and structured approach. A potential sale involves a complex set of issues. While macro economic conditions are largely beyond the Board's control, considerations around strategy, management, local markets and community implications are not. However, addressing these factors, in the context of dynamic strategic reviews, can be challenging.

Engaging management in a dialogue around strategic options can be a delicate matter as the Board works to promote shareholder interests while balancing the potential perception of conflict between the community, employees and senior management's own interests.

One regional bank Board found its answer by engaging the management team in a series of strategic workshops, aimed at a frank assessment of the company's strategic opportunities. Here's what they did:

1. ***Get the real story:*** In preparing for the initial workshop, management and directors completed an anonymous survey that assessed perceptions of the company's strengths and weaknesses, corporate culture, organization and management style, key challenges and opportunities. As it turned out, the survey revealed significant convergence of thought between directors and senior management, but it also exposed distinct areas of difference between the groups.

2. ***Get everyone talking the same language:*** The survey results, and differences in perception among Board members and management, were discussed in a joint workshop. External benchmarks, other banks' experiences, peer group and best practice strategies were added to the mix, resulting in a constructive, fact-based dialogue examining key strategic paths. As an outcome of the workshop, management was tasked with developing a "blueprint" for implementing the key, agreed strategic drivers.

3. ***Develop a Blueprint:*** Management engaged the organization in an interactive process, and 400 discrete action programs were developed to enable realization of the strategic objectives. Action programs were in-depth, granular descriptions of enablers that made the strategy come to life, and were established within each line of business. For instance, within the consumer bank, action plans addressed criteria for balancing de-novo branches against whole institution acquisitions, defined banking center staff core competencies and addressed talent gaps, and developed relationship-based product packages and sales programs.

4. ***Refine the Blueprint:*** The Board engaged with management in a two-day strategy review where key aspects of the plan were refined. Directors and managers continued their open dialogue as they examined the various key enablers.

5. ***Implement the strategy and assess results:*** As the strategy is being implemented, the Board will receive regular updates and independently assess whether the results meet the objectives and whether a course of continued independence is warranted.

   Following this structured approach to asking hard questions and developing a measurable set of enablers to deliver its strategy, the bank's Board and management are able to develop jointly a vision that the organization can rally around.

While undertaking this approach, the regional bank and its directors and management team have become an independent, aggressive acquiring team (asset size has more than doubled since the effort started). More than ever, they share a vision of the future, and as a result, they are better equipped to decide if, at any point, an offer comes along that is simply too good to refuse. More likely, though, they will be among the ones making the offers as the banking industry continues its consolidation.

"Aston Associates was a natural choice for First Niagara when we were evaluating our opportunities in the midst of the financial crisis. Ever since we partnered with Aston in 2004 to develop our Strategic Blueprint, we have found them to be an invaluable advisor.

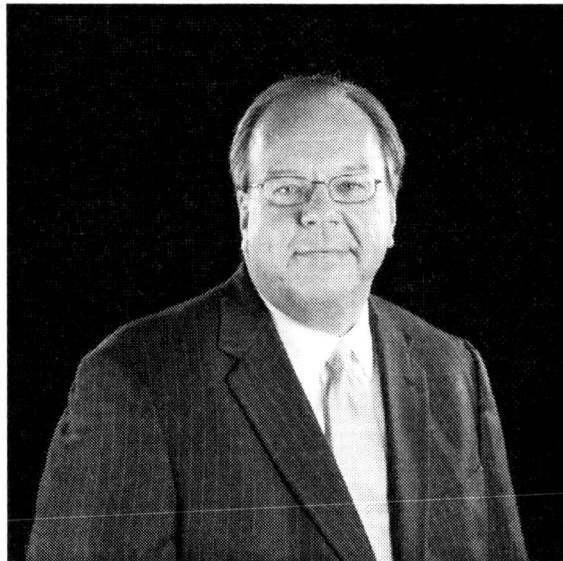

In 2009, Aston has helped us reevaluate our strategy in light of the changing economic environment; organize our due diligence efforts around two transformative acquisitions combining for 140 branches and $8.3 billion in deposits, and drive the integrations of both of the acquired entities. Aston's knowledge of the financial services arena; their expertise in evaluating and structuring transactions; and their ability to adapt to the changing environment are absolutely indispensible."

John R. Koelmel

Chief Executive Officer

First Niagara Financial Group

Buffalo, New York

In Busy M&A Generation, Few Deals Brought Value Promised

*Article originally published in American Banker on
October 26, 2001*

Reprinted with permission

After two decades of brisk consolidation, bankers are generally taking a step back to focus on creating value from the acquisitions they made rather than making more purchases.

Between 1989 and 1999, the number of U.S. banks shrunk by a little more than 40%, but merger-and-acquisition activity slowed considerably in 2001. In the first half of the year there were 108 bank and thrift deals; there were 141 in the second half of 2000. Deal values fell 59%, and the amount of assets changing hands fell 62%.

What is being discovered during this pause? First, that few institutions have delivered the value they forecast when they announced their deals. Second, that where organizations have reaped full financial, operational, and shareholder benefits, there had been a rigorous analysis and implementation process.

In many mergers the acquirer finds itself unable to deliver the projected efficiencies, earnings, and shareholder benefits. The market's skepticism of bank acquisitions can be found almost daily in the media, and it appears this skepticism is well grounded.

In a 1998 review, Federal Reserve members Steven Pilloff and Anthony Santomero argued that mergers that year yielded little benefit or none at all, and that the combined company's market value was, on average, no higher than the value of its parts.

In a fourth-quarter-1999 update on banking mergers by the Federal Reserve Bank of Atlanta, Simon Kwan and Robert Eisenbeis found that more than half of the performance variables they studied declined postmerger: there was a shift from positive to negative in the mean ROE based on operating income in the eight quarters that followed the merger; and the mean efficiency ratio postmerger fell by a marginal 0.34%.

Clearly, acquirers' ability to capture anticipated synergies of expense efficiency and market benefit is mixed at best.

There are, however, examples of organizations that delivered on their promises. One that has shown exceptional ability to build shareholder value through acquisition over the past decade is the institution now known as U.S. Bancorp. Under the leadership of Jerry Grundhofer, the Minneapolis company has grown from $7 billion of assets in 1992 to $209 billion today, and has essentially doubled its asset size every two years since 1997.

With each acquisition, U.S. Bancorp has managed its efficiency ratio downward — from a high in 1992 of 63% to a low of 44% . The compound annual growth rate of its stock price from 1992 to 2000 was 29%, compared with 16% for the Standard & Poor's bank index. These outstanding results are driven by management that continually challenges its leaders to identify the specific opportunities in each acquisition and ensures that they are achieved.

So how does a bank address the market's initial skepticism and effectively wring the full potential out of a combined entity following an acquisition? We see four critical steps:

Identify clear leadership. The CEO must take control over crucial dependencies, make tough decisions, and be prepared to spend a lot of time executing the consolidation plan.

It's important to get all levels of the organization involved. The first step in this process is to appoint executives from all the business lines to an integration group responsible for prioritizing issues and coordinating efforts.

This group should direct eight to ten teams of high-performing individuals who involve content experts in identifying integration and revenue opportunities and monitoring implementation progress. The CEO must work quickly to choose participants and communicate how integration will be planned and carried out. Without this control and decisiveness, there is a real risk that critical time will be wasted with senior management vying for positions in the new organization.

Establish an adequate due diligence process and set savings and revenue goals high. Lack of a sound due diligence process creates the danger of overstating or understating the value of the merger, can weaken the buyer's asset base, and can cause managers to generalize in speaking of revenue and efficiencies. There must be specificity that will lead to externally announced goals and objectives. On the expense side, due diligence should allow the organization to accurately identify the consolidation of information technology systems, back-office operations, salespeople's roles, administrative support structures, and distribution outlets.

On the revenue side, customer attrition management is essential. When Bank of America entered the Florida market by acquiring Barnett Banks Inc., it discovered that the customer attrition level peaked at a loss of 4,000 savings and checking accounts per month on a net basis. Over time this represented a 7% decline in market share and 16% drop in profitability from 1998 levels. Now, because of a combination of a new, customer-centric product set and sales incentives, Bank of America reports an average of 3,800 to 4,000 net new savings and checking accounts per month.

Setting high targets will bring out creativity in the integration design and motivate managers, resulting in a service and product approach that meets customers' perceived value and is delivered through efficient, streamlined mechanisms.

Redesign rather than integrate. Many institutions have difficulty in integrating an acquisition and achieving the prerequisite integration economies. Consolidation provides an opportunity to step back and look at both merger partners' processes, infrastructure, and business approaches instead of simply migrating potentially inefficient processes from the acquirer on to the target. This does not mean the institutions should attempt to take the best practices of both organizations and create the perfect bank. The new organization will not be perfect. However, fixing the parts before forming the whole can be done in such a way as to capture the redesign potential of the individual banks and bring more value to the new entity.

Develop a comprehensive communications plan. In the 2001 *American Banker* / Gallup Consumer Survey, 54% of customers whose banks had been involved in a merger over the past year had an unfavorable opinion about the deal. The mitigating factor most often cited by industry leaders was open and ongoing communication with the customer. Evidence of the effect is clear, with BB&T, which has been involved in more than 45 mergers in the last decade, retaining 97% of its customers.

In the same regard, a structured and continuous communications plan that promotes participation among employees and keeps them informed will ease some of the inevitable anxiety and prepare them for customers' questions about the merger.

Regardless of where the acquiring bank is in the consolidation process, a comprehensive redesign — one that focuses on examining processes, infrastructure and the business approaches driving revenues — will alleviate operational duplication, create real economies of scale, and generate super-normal revenue growth from realigned products and services that ultimately benefit employees, customers, and shareholders.

> *"With support from Aston, not only were the employees' ideas implemented, they were the ones who implemented them."*

Oliver Waddell

Chairman and Chief Executive Officer (Ret)

Star Banc (now U.S. Bancorp)

Cincinnati, Ohio

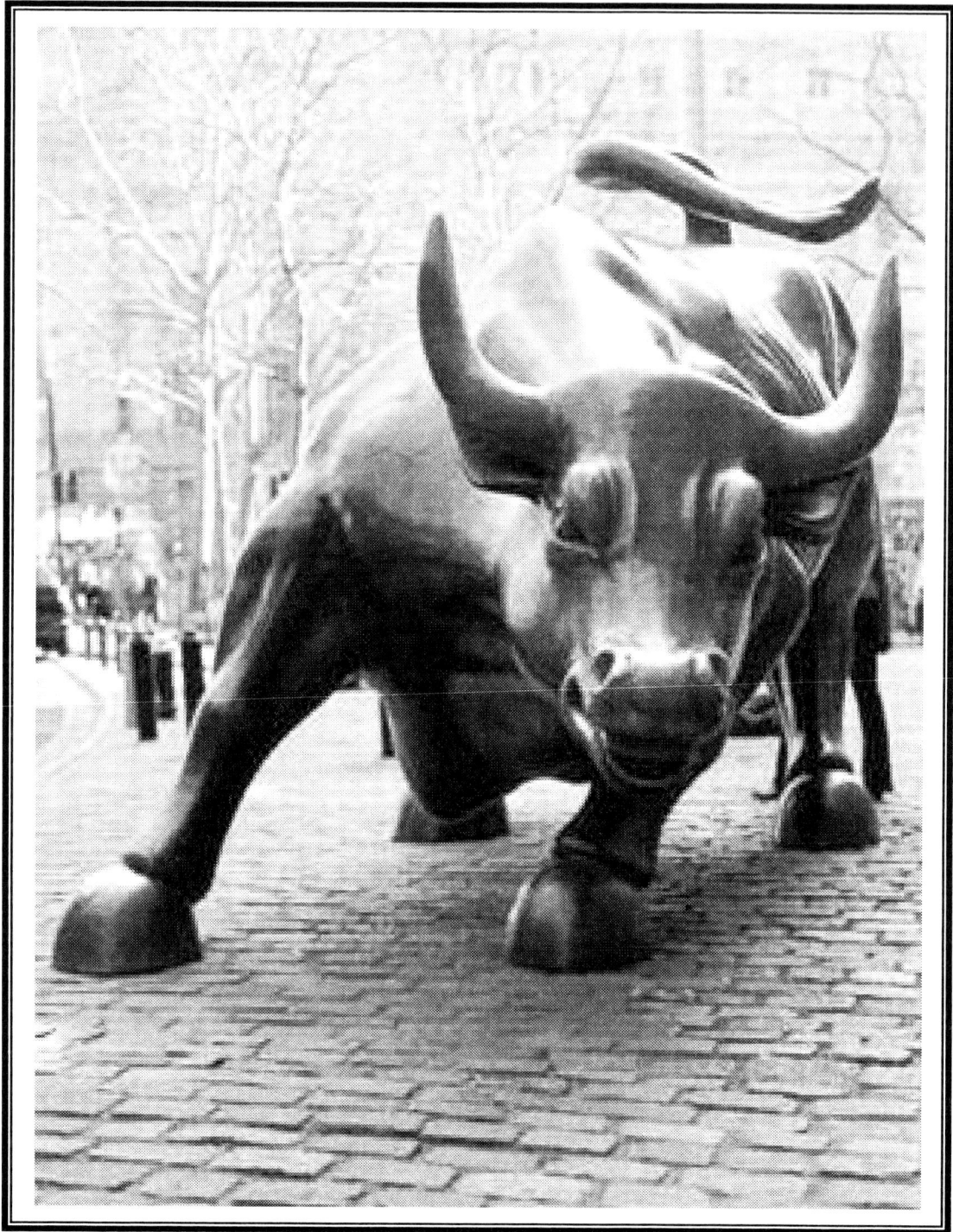

Chapter Three

RIDING INDUSTRY TRENDS TO POSITION FOR COMPETITIVE OUTPERFORMANCE

Chapter 3 Introduction

Riding industry trends to position for competitive out-performance has taken many forms over the years. We have worked with banks facing virtually every stage of interest rate, real estate and business cycles. Meeting challenges and thriving as a result of shifts in external conditions are integral to successful risk management and, ultimately, bank performance management.

As the industry in 2010 faces a challenging rate environment, a defaulting real estate sector, higher funding costs, wide-spread credit and capital adequacy concerns and heightened regulatory pressure, being agile and able to respond to changes in external conditions is more important than ever.

In the last ten years, bank-distributed insurance has grown at an annual rate of 27%. Most, if not all, banks have already decided that they will sell insurance and are now considering how best to do so.

Despite the soft property-casualty market and tough economy, the nation's bank holding companies (BHCs) experienced an increase of 38.5 percent in their total insurance revenue from $10.88 billion in 2008 to a record $15.08 billion in 2009.

Among the top 50 in insurance revenue, the mean ratio of the concentration of total insurance revenue to noninterest income was 16.4 percent in 2009. Among the top 50 in this Concentration Ratio, the mean was 46.6 percent.

However, the rate environment and the economic recession have severely impacted top line growth and bank-owned agency value during the past 18 months. For the twelve months ending 6/30/09, the average total return on prior year value of a bank-owned insurance agency was a negative 10.2%.

For most agencies, value deflation was impacted by a steep reduction in "other income" (contingent income, supplemental income and investment income). The key difference between the best and the worst, however, was a direct result of poor management. Over the past 24 months, many bank-owned agencies have implemented short-term cost saving initiatives in hopes of preserving profitability, but instead destroyed organic growth and long-term sustainability.

In "Get the Cross-Sell You Bought the Agency For" we examine the market for bank-distributed insurance in the US, and offer ideas for what to do and not to do.

We wrote "Erosion of Lazy Money Can Be Deadly to the Slothful" just as the tide of the "new economy" was starting to ebb and illustrated the power of relying on fact-based analysis and structured assessment of strategic options as the superior basis for making decisions and driving performance. Nothing could be more true in today's challenging operating environment.

Source: Mortgage Bankers Association

U.S. Banks Play Significantly Less of a Role in Insurance Sales Than Banks in Other Markets

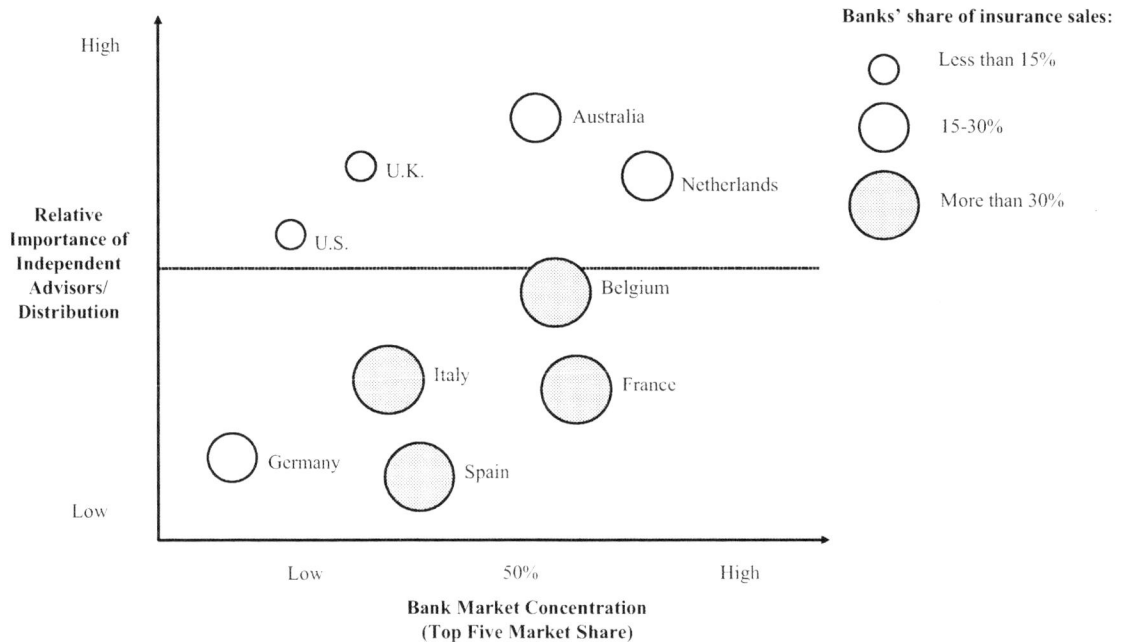

Source: Corporate Executive Board, Group of Ten, "Report on Consolidation in the Financial Sector," ABN-AMRO

> *"Aston Associates helped us improve all aspects of our organization, and did so with passion, knowledge and intelligence."*

David Gall

Group Executive, Retail Business

St. George Bank

Sydney, Australia

Get the Cross-Sell You Bought the Agency For

*Article originally published in American Banker on
March 18, 2006*

Reprinted with permission

Bank-owned agencies play an increasingly important role in distribution of insurance products

From 1999 to 2003 bank-owned premiums increased at a compound annual rate of 21%, to $78 billion, according to an *American Banker's* Insurance Association study. The number of bank holding companies reporting insurance revenue rose 11%, to 1,413, and the revenue itself climbed 22%, to a record $41 billion.

Top 50 Bank Holding Companies Earned 94% of All Insurance Income Earned by Banks

$ million total insurance income YTD June 30, 2005

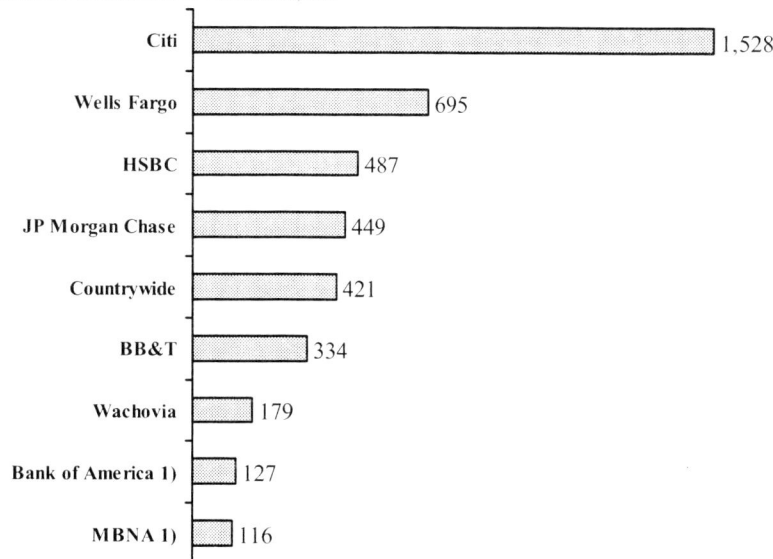

Citi	1,528
Wells Fargo	695
HSBC	487
JP Morgan Chase	449
Countrywide	421
BB&T	334
Wachovia	179
Bank of America 1)	127
MBNA 1)	116

1)   Bank of America and MBNA have signed definite agreement to merge.
Source: American Bankers Insurance Association, Bankinsurance.com

This robust growth is largely the result of aggressive acquisition. The top five M&A advisers facilitated 361 bank/agency deals from 1999 to 2004. Banks owned 25% of the top 40 insurance brokers by 2003.

With insurance carriers focusing on reducing distribution costs and regulators scrutinizing commission structures, many independent agents have come to view sale to a bank as their best recourse. They think of banks as strategic buyers willing to pay two or three times revenue, though in 2003 only 13% of the premiums in such deals were larger than two times revenue.

Banks have bought insurance agencies to add stability and strength to non-interest income and diversify their offerings to increase wallet share. The trend is likely to continue. According to the ABIA study, 86% of banks that bought insurance agencies said they met or exceeded financial projections. — ? No Way!

diagram.

A Growing Share of Banks Offer Insurance

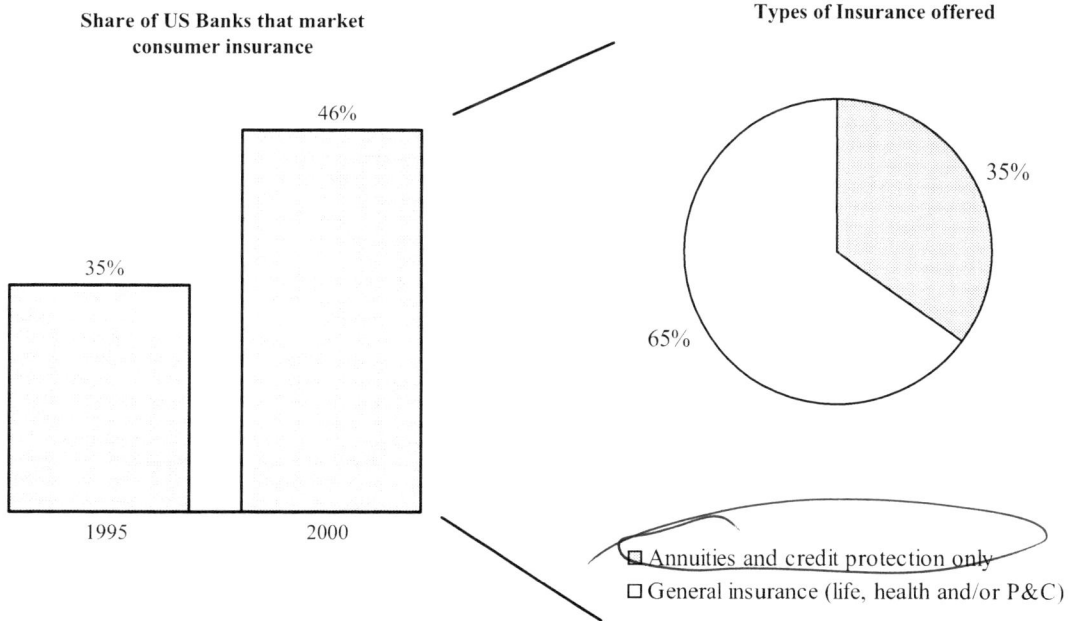

Share of US Banks that market consumer insurance

Types of Insurance offered

46%

35%

35%

65%

1995   2000

☐ Annuities and credit protection only
☐ General insurance (life, health and/or P&C)

Sources: Dumm & Hoyt presentation to International Insurance Society, 2002, Association of Banks in Insurance

The fit of insurance with personal and commercial lending is obvious. New mortgages, cars, and commercial facilities all require insurance policies. By offering insurance concurrently, the bank is helping clients protect these assets.

But the cross-selling potential has proved difficult to realize. According to a 2004 benchmarking study by Reagan Consulting, revenue from cross-selling typically made up only 5% to 8% of bank-owned agencies' total — and in some cases as little as 2%. Only 1% of the owner banks' commercial lending customers had been cross-sold property and casualty insurance. For retail banking households, the figure was less than 0.5%. Cross-sale penetration of life and health policies was even lower. Though some claim modest success in insurance cross-selling, for most results are dismal. The main reasons are a clash of corporate cultures and lack of trust.

Insurance agency producers and principals, frustrated by bank bureaucracy and mediocre sales skills, quickly adjust back to their "independent" model. They interact with the bank only enough to justify the deal premium through back-office synergies.

The culture clash can seem insurmountable. Agents used to being big fish in their pond find bankers stoic and blinkered by rules and procedures. Commercial lenders, branch platform staff, and mortgage originators tend to view the "insurance folks" as slick, shallow salespeople with limited respect for banks' customer-service culture.

Concerns about licensing requirements for insurance product sales and regulatory barriers against discounting and bundling insurance and non-insurance products further widen the cultural gap. After buying an agency, one regional bank encouraged its branch staff to solicit customers for insurance needs and provided a monetary incentive for referrals. Referrals flooded the agency — but turned out to be 98% nonqualified. The result: a massive workload and a near-zero success rate.

The referrals could not be acted on in a meaningful way because branch customers had unacceptable risk profiles or policies whose cancellation penalties outweighed the benefits of switching. Though agency employees understood the importance of expiration dates, branch employees did not.

The agency employees quickly decided that the bank's clients were not worth pursuing. The branch employees concluded that the insurance people were unwilling or unable to help bank customers, and that referring them only strained the customer relationship.

A structured approach to assessing such culture gaps can help to overcome them. The analysis must take place at the time of acquisition, and common operating processes must be established at the start. Opportunities to align and integrate back-office, call center, and account-management functions must be carefully examined. Putting agency and bank employees in the same location can pay off in efficiency and in cultural terms.

Some banks sidestep the cultural issues so as not to endanger a deal. The effect can be entrenched cultural challenges and associated costs.

The key strategic drivers of the bank's operating philosophy must be mirrored in the acquired insurance agency. For example, if the bank intends to be customer-centric, the insurance agency should not be product-centric. The bank and the agency must also synchronize in customer segmentation. Otherwise, there is little chance of meaningful cross-selling.

Through a structured review, one regional bank found a solution to the branch referral experiment gone awry. Rather than reward branch employees for referrals, it rewarded them for collecting information about customers' insurance policies — for example, expiration and carrier. Armed with this information, the agency could target customers as renewal approached and offer value-added policy reviews as well as a chance for a better deal by shopping among carriers. This approach, backed by a sales-management tool that actively tracked referrals, leads, and follow-ups, helped build confidence on both sides of the fence and enabled the agency to boost its personal lines premiums by 20% in the first year alone.

Erosion of Lazy Money Can Be Deadly to the Slothful

Article originally published in American Banker on May 18, 2001

Reprinted with permission

Rational human behavior would dictate that customers move their checking, savings, CDs, and credit products to Internet banks, national credit card houses, and top brokerage firms if they offer better terms than banks.

Yet, to date, regional banks have been remarkably insulated from lazy money erosion. In fact, many regional banks would be out of business today if it were not for the ability to hang onto such money.

The specter of lazy money erosion is increasingly difficult to ignore, however. According to a study by the New York consulting firm Novantas quoted in *American Banker* ["Aggregation Revenue-Drain Pegged at $28B for Banks,"], banks could lose up to $28 billion of revenue to customers' moving their money to accounts to earn more interest or higher returns. In fact as a % of total personal financial assets, currency and deposits has declined from 35.7% to 15.4% from 1977 to 2002 (see figure next page).

**Personal-Sector Financial Asset Holdings:
Percentage of Total - 1977**

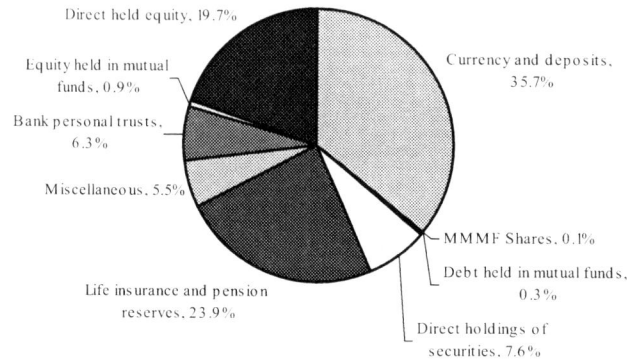

Direct held equity, 19.7%

Equity held in mutual funds, 0.9%

Bank personal trusts, 6.3%

Miscellaneous, 5.5%

Currency and deposits, 35.7%

MMMF Shares, 0.1%

Debt held in mutual funds, 0.3%

Direct holdings of securities, 7.6%

Life insurance and pension reserves, 23.9%

**Personal-Sector Financial Asset Holdings:
Percentage of Total - 2002**

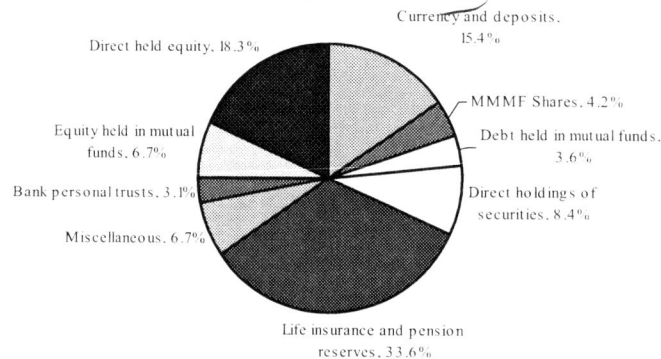

Currency and deposits, 15.4%

Direct held equity, 18.3%

Equity held in mutual funds, 6.7%

Bank personal trusts, 3.1%

Miscellaneous, 6.7%

MMMF Shares, 4.2%

Debt held in mutual funds, 3.6%

Direct holdings of securities, 8.4%

Life insurance and pension reserves, 33.6%

Source: Federal Reserve

Regional bank managers must face this challenge or they will be at greater risk than ever of serious revenue erosion over the next three to five years.

Here are the threats:

The technology revolution continues. Despite the dot-com meltdown, online bill payment, statements, and account consolidation are increasingly becoming the preferred way to transact and manage finances. Technology also continues to open doors to new entrants. The emergence of internet portals with aggregation capabilities, internet-only banks and discount banks, and sophisticated on-line research providers such as Morningstar, is increasingly forcing banks to offer more sophisticated products and services.

Generation X and the Baby Boomer effect. While the values of Generation X have already changed the demand for financial services, it is the adoption of the internet as a viable and acceptable delivery channel by the Baby Boomers that has accelerated the pace of change. 40% of U.S. households now have access to high speed internet connections. The generation shift has not yet affected the "A-customer" (top 20% profitability) demographics of most banks, causing a deceptive "calm before the storm." Moreover, on the one hand financial institutions will be faced with the ever greater demands from Generation X to deliver financial information through a broader spectrum of access points as internet access becomes more ubiquitous (e.g., through merging technologies such as phones, PDAs, and PCs). On the other, the demands of the Baby Boomers will create more pressure on financial services firms to offer best-of-breed product capabilities whether proprietary or through third parties to satisfy the growing financial needs of this group as they near retirement.

Cherry-pickers attack from both sides. Fueled by cheaper cost structures, online brokerage and internet-only banks are cherry-picking technology-savvy customers. Former niche players such as ING, Schwab, Fidelity, and E-Trade have become household names. Also, some large financial institutions have the brand value, which regional banks lack, to attract the top-end trust and private

This double squeeze may leave regional banks "stuck in the middle," with primarily higher-cost and lower-value clients.

Pop culture embraces bank-bashing. As a result of poorly guided and badly communicated fee increases, bank-bashing has increasingly become a favorite pastime for the public and press. The intensity of unfavorable press attacks has increased dramatically as banks rely more heavily on fees.

Banks should begin actively addressing this challenge along five main dimensions:

Establish baseline and tracking methodology. Effectively monitoring changes in customers' behavior is remarkably undervalued in banks' executive suites as a way to recognize and stem the movement of lazy money. Tracking shifts and changes from a defined baseline can shed remarkable insights on what is and what is not happening across the employee and customer base.

Understand customer elasticity and price-to-value. Most banks still have, at best, a rudimentary understanding of the value customers place on their various products and services. Understanding and adjusting prices in accordance with value to customers is crucial, but banks rarely focus their best resources on it. Those that do are more likely to succeed. Banks must continuously review, update, and enhance what customers value to maintain value-pricing momentum, and avoid the need for one-time, unsustainable efforts.

Build exit barriers. By adding direct deposit and debits and cross-selling insurance and card products, bank managers are trying to build effective barriers to customer defection. In essence they are trying to keep money lazy.

In the words of one regional bank chief executive officer: "Retain your A-customers, cross-sell your B-customers, and minimize the efforts on behalf of your C-customers."

A segmented approach ensures sound investment of your resources.

Use technology to enhance sales and service. As other, leaner business models drive the overall cost structure of the financial services industry down, banks need to lower their operational expenses to maintain market position.

Recruit and develop dynamic talent. Some observers claim that most banks continue to attract safety-seeking employees. Though such observations are oversimplified, they go to the core of an issue at many bank: their fondness for the current state. Admittedly, taking care of lazy money has not traditionally attracted the highest-energy talent. But banks cannot succeed without addressing this issue. Regional banks simply cannot continue to count on lazy money staying lazy. The $28 billion risk of revenue erosion and shareholder value destruction is too high.

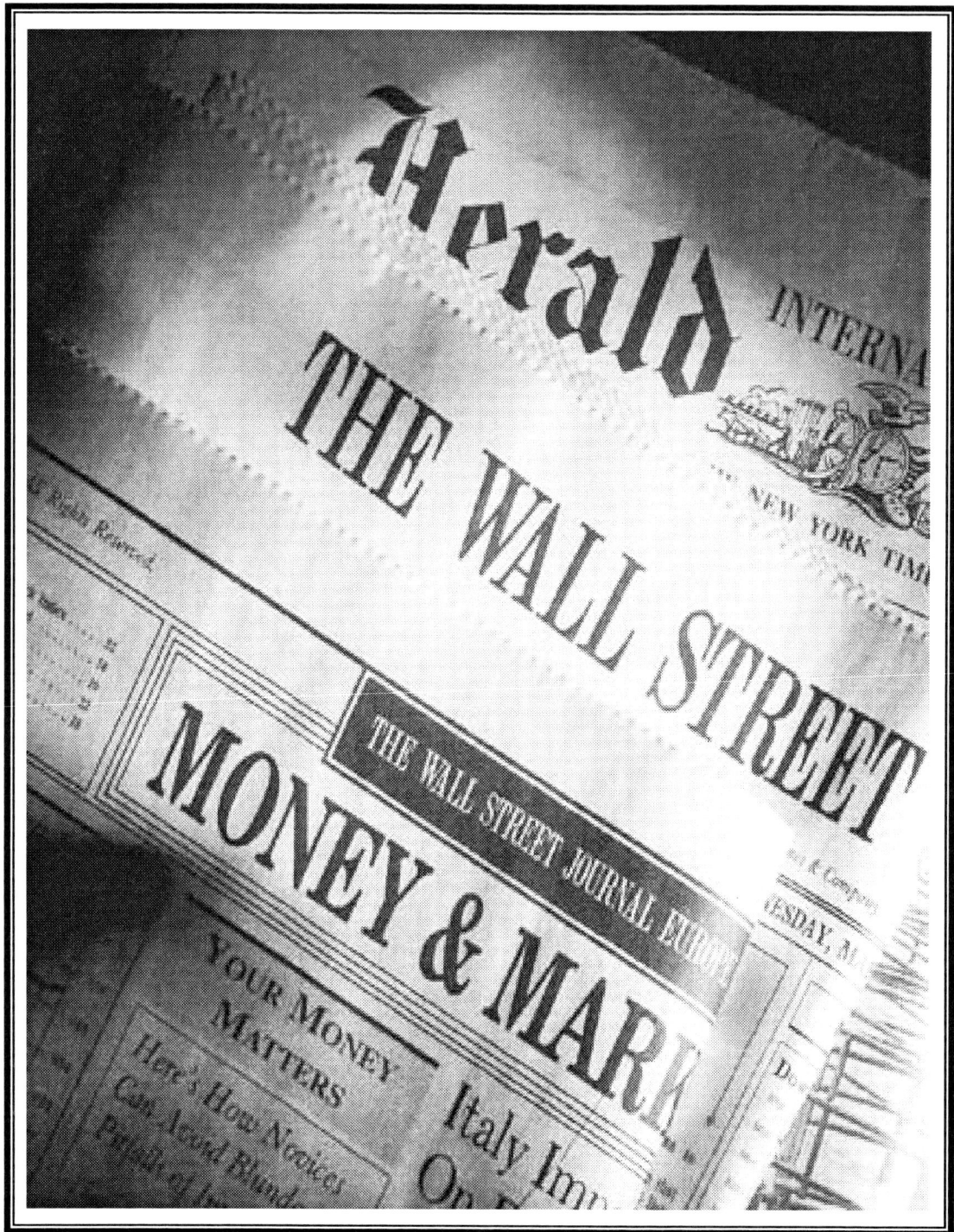

OPTIMIZING
NON-INTEREST
INCOME

Chapter 4 Introduction

We have championed the theme of "Optimizing non-interest income" for nearly 20 years and sometimes have been met with expressions of disbelief. For many banks, lack of attention to non-interest income reflects the relatively limited role non-interest income plays on their income statement. Also, for some, non-interest income translates to "non-banking" businesses like insurance and investments.

The problem, of course, is that historically, non-interest income opportunities rarely get the focus or rigor they deserve, and as a result, are often woefully under-managed — until now.

The banking industry generated nearly $40 billion from fees on deposits in 2008, about $5 billion more than just three years earlier. Service charges on overdrafts were a leading contributor to the welcome boost in fee income in the face of steep losses on the lending side of many banks' businesses.

Consumer groups and lawmakers — spurred to regulate banks' business decisions because the government has pumped more than $700 billion into the ailing financial sector — pushed hard for legislation that will put strict, permanent limits on overdraft charges and debit card fees as part of the financial reform bill.

We believe there are tried and true fundamental tactics which can be strategically implemented to effectively mitigate the impact of the new legislation and successfully offset anticipated losses.

Source: SNL Financial

In "Going After Fee Income Takes Sophisticated Strategy," we examine some of the options banks should consider to ensure appropriate focus on this area.

In "Elasticity: the Forgotten Component of Pricing," we illustrate the importance of recognizing the relationship between expected relative change in demand and change in price. Considering it "too difficult to measure," many banks still do not include elasticity in their pricing models.

Finally, a series of three articles published in *American Banker* contains a comprehensive review of banks' non-interest pricing challenges and opportunities. This series examines the critical importance of recognizing "perceived customer value" when assessing non-interest pricing. In today's "free checking" deposit environment and "all establishment fees waived" on loans, these articles provide critical insights when looking for innovative non-interest income opportunities.

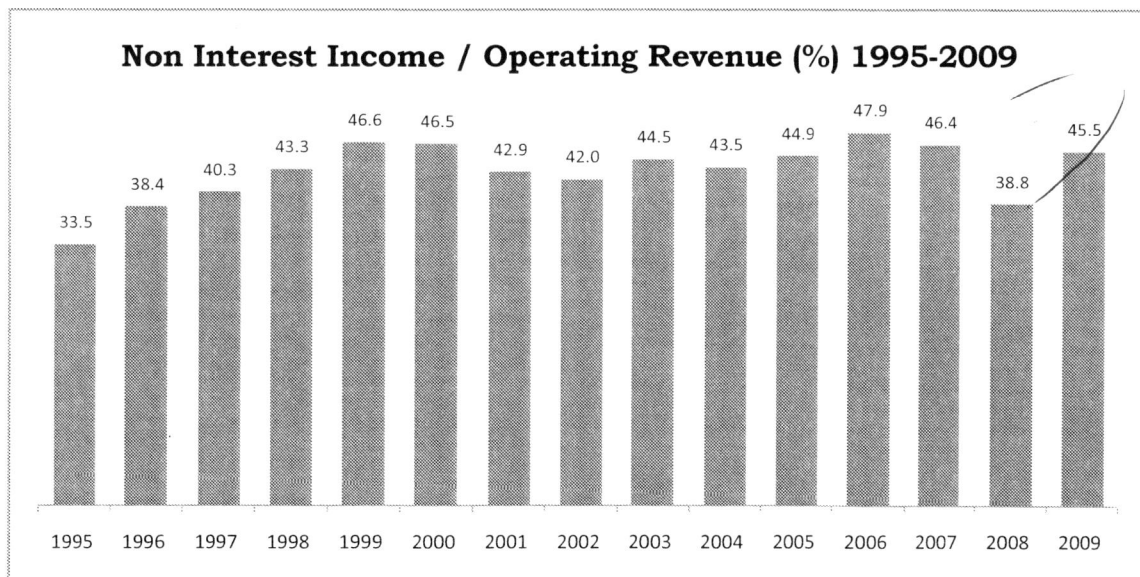

Non Interest Income / Operating Revenue (%) 1995-2009

Year	Value
1995	33.5
1996	38.4
1997	40.3
1998	43.3
1999	46.6
2000	46.5
2001	42.9
2002	42.0
2003	44.5
2004	43.5
2005	44.9
2006	47.9
2007	46.4
2008	38.8
2009	45.5

Going After Fee Income Takes Sophisticated Strategy

Originally published in American Banker January 5, 2001

Reprinted with permission

With fee income growing as a portion of banks' income statements, focused non-interest income strategies are becoming increasingly critical in maintaining growth. However, very few banks apply the level of scrutiny and sophistication to non-interest income sources that they do to loan and deposit income. This commentary argues that winning banks over the next decade will succeed in building and realizing customer value through a superior fee income approach.

Non-interest income growth has been a key driver of shareholder value creation in the last 5 years

By increasingly relying on non-interest income, banks have dramatically raised fees and grown fee-based businesses in recent years. With a 15% compound annual growth rate recently, non-interest income has grown to 43% of total revenue for US commercial banks. This in comparison with 40% in Australia, 33% in northern Europe and 13% in Japan – clearly US banks have leveraged the benefits of non-interest income more than their international counterparts. In the Federal Reserve's annual report to Congress on banking fees, the message has been consistent over the last three years: banking fees are going up.

This year's report concluded that the level of fees at banks increased significantly in nine of twenty-one cases examined. Last year, the Federal Reserve reported that bank fees increased significantly in six of twenty cases examined.

Figure: Non-Interest Income as Percent of Total Revenue

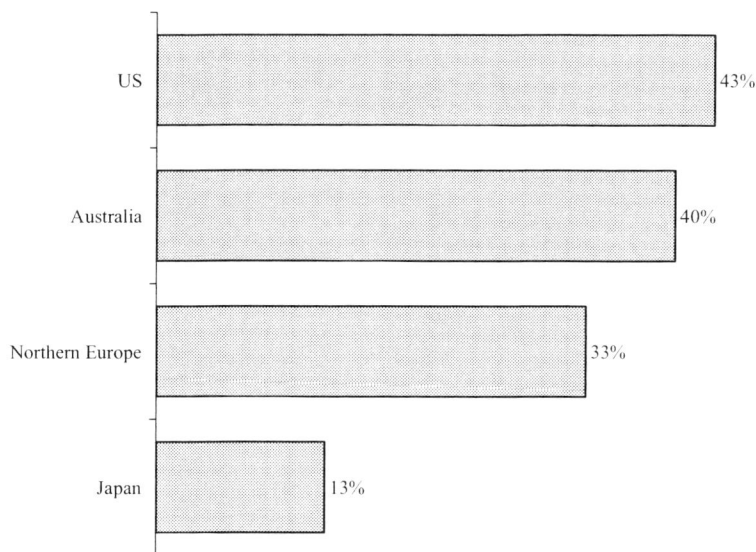

Source: Aston Analysis

Strategies committed to increasing non-interest income have long been applauded by Wall Street. Bank of New York has become an analyst favorite on the strength of its continued non-interest income performance. With 63% of third quarter 2000 revenue generated from non-interest income, Bank of New York commands a P/E ratio of approximately 30. This represents twice the industry average. A regression analysis comparing P/E ratios and the non-interest income portion of total income shows a remarkably high degree of fit. In fact, the results from looking at the top 50 banks in the US indicate that a 5% increase in non-interest income as a percentage of total income is consistent with a 2 point higher P/E ratio. Despite this, many banks treat non-interest income as peripheral to their core strategy, not giving it the attention nor applying the tools required for its long-term growth.

If the last five years' growth in non-interest income is any indication of the future, 55-60% of total revenue for commercial banks will likely come from non-interest sources by 2011. Do US bankers have the skill sct and application required to manage this?

There are five sources of concern for the future of non-interest growth: 1) media-driven customer backlash, 2) accelerating legal and regulatory interest, 3) "lose-lose" strategies, 4) geographic limitations and 5) customer behavior impact

1. Media-driven customer backlash

It is an odd paradox that customers are relatively price inelastic (versus service quality, for example) for price increases on service attributes they value, yet become highly annoyed by penny-pinching fees. Largely as a result of poorly guided and under-developed fee increase initiatives that are badly communicated, bank bashing has become a favorite pastime for the public and press. The intensity of negative press coverage has increased dramatically as banks continue to rely more heavily on fees and customer backlash resulting from negative press is becoming more of a threat to banks. Media stories range from the battle over ATM fees in Santa Monica to disgruntled customers on both coasts debating inactivity fees, minimum balance requirements, account maintenance charges and returned-check fees.

2. Accelerating legal and regulatory interest

Customer backlash over non-interest income has also made its way to the courts and state houses in recent years. From ATM surcharge fee struggles in California to the proposed "bank fee fairness measure" in Massachusetts, costly legal and regulatory battles are challenging banks' ability to realize non-interest income growth. Providian, Citigroup and Chase are among high-profile banks that have settled class action lawsuits over card division fees in 2000, with estimated settlement amounts of $300 million, $45 million and $7 million, respectively. Add attorney fees, lost fee income and cost of additional customer notification to the settlement amounts and you have an enormous legal bill for the year. As banks' non-interest revenue continues to be scrutinized, defensibility of pricing strategies will likely become increasingly important.

3. "Lose-lose" strategies

Non-interest income growth prospects are also being put at risk by banks using unconventional tactics to gain attention and market share. While the general trend continues to be price increases across the industry, exceptions are reported almost on a daily basis. Commerce Bancorp received coverage in the Wall Street Journal this year for its fast-food-inspired pricing approach; while Washington Mutual's decision to remove foreign ATM fees in California received editorial praise in the San Francisco Chronicle. However, as any banker with an understanding of classic game theory would know, if others follow this strategy, the outcome is inevitably a lose-lose situation for all banks involved.

One banking sector that has consistently exploited low-fee strategies over the last five years is internet banking, offering no fee, high interest accounts to attract initial market share. Exclusively internet banks as well as brick-and-mortar bank internet divisions have all jumped on this band-wagon. The case for the business model remains to be proven, however. NetBank is reportedly operating with a ROA of .02% (vs. peer average 0.98%) and an efficiency ratio of 97.11% (vs. peer average 57%). This is hardly sustainable long term.

4. Geographic limitations

There appears to be little consistency and targeting for strategies in fee pricing throughout the country. Why do consumers in Florida pay 200% more in monthly account keeping fees than consumers in Indiana? How come the five highest checking fees are in Alabama, Oklahoma, Florida, Georgia and Texas; all five states that have lower-than-average cost-of-living? Why are banking fees in Arizona, Washington and Minnesota among the lowest in the nation, when these are states where bank consolidation is at its highest? The significant variances across regions certainly suggest that a majority of banks may not optimize local market opportunities. Although multi-state institutions generally charge significantly higher fees than single-state institutions, important exceptions to this rule exist. Minimum balances required to open NOW, statement savings and checking accounts are on average lower by 42%, 29% and 15%, respectively, for multi-state institutions than for single-state institutions, suggesting that the larger players have recognized and responded to the relatively high elasticity/ sensitivity customers have to balance thresholds. Combined with wide distribution and teaser pricing, the lower thresholds enable larger institutions to attract customers, despite overall competitive fee levels. Conversely, low elasticity fees like stop-payment orders, overdraft and NSF charges were higher by 38%, 33% and 28%, respectively, at multi-state institutions compared to single state institutions last year, suggesting that fee income growth potential exists for single state institutions.

5. Customer behavior impact

Finally, there is emerging evidence that unsophisticated fee increases have limited positive total revenue impact. A study by the Federal Reserve in 2000 concluded that pure price increases on checking accounts generally resulted in neutral or lower bank revenues when taking into account the effect of customers reducing their deposit levels. Only check return and NSF fees were found to significantly raise checking account revenues (with a one percent fee increase resulting in a 1.3% and a 3.7% net revenue increase, respectively). In other words, increased fees do not necessarily equal increased total revenues or bottom-line improvement when they are not linked to perceived customer value.

Opportunities still abound for sophisticated fee strategies by taking a fact-based, structured approach: 1) establish pricing baseline and analyze current state, 2) identify new pricing opportunities, and 3) monitor and track implementation

1. Establish pricing baseline and analyze current state

Most banks have at best a broad understanding of what drives their non-interest income. Establishing the starting point for each line of business, (cleansed of non-controllable and non-recurring items) is a key step often ignored. Lacking facts, fee changes are often implemented based on perception and a "match the bank across the street" methodology. Understanding the current state is inevitably more complicated, however, and is the key to unlocking non-interest income potential. Only by conducting unit-cost pricing analysis at the micro level does the bank truly understand its cost of a particular product line. One regional bank found that 2 of 3 deposit products were negative contributors, requiring a complete overhaul of the product offering. Product attribute ranking and customer value analysis helps identify "pockets of value" not currently recognized. A major Australian bank found that several attributes of its corner stone commercial lending products were dramatically under-priced when compared to the value of these attributes. Elasticity analysis reveals evidence of pricing mistakes and opportunities alike. A western regional bank found an opportunity to eliminate a particularly elastic fee, and as a result gained great volume and public relations benefit. Fee waiver and exemption analysis typically indicates employee practices in stark contrast to official policy, with non-collection of fees as high as 70%. Risk and run-off analysis enables product managers and business leaders to assess likely competitive and customer reaction to any change. In sum, this set of analyses paints a robust picture of current reality, enabling focus on growth opportunities.

2. *Identify new pricing opportunities*

International markets suggest non-interest income sources that have yet to be tapped in the US. Along with new product development, new pricing opportunities are greatly underestimated by US banks. Australian and European banks both enjoy very significant fee sources in their lending markets yet untouched by the majority of US banking institutions (e.g. loan administration fees on residential and non-card consumer loans represent as much as 80% of total consumer lending fees at one Australian bank). Similarly, with the maturing of on-line banking programs (as evidenced in the more mature Scandinavian markets), new non-interest income opportunities (eg. transaction, account keeping and opening/closing fees) are created in this area as well. Both sources, largely untouched by the US banking industry, will continue to grow in importance as the nature of these services continues to develop. The key for US bankers is to keep "eyes and ears open," and anticipate and recognize these opportunities as they present themselves.

3. *Monitor and track implementation*

Active monitoring and tracking of fee initiatives is a requirement that most tend to ignore. One regional bank instituted a procedure for reviewing proposed fee initiatives, but kept no record of the market reception, customer run-off and behavior changes, thus getting no value from this process. Another regional bank decided to launch a series of fee increases in one division, not recognizing the impact this would have on other divisions, ultimately resulting in a net loss to the organization. The positive impact of monitoring and tracking is that "what gets measured gets done." One regional bank introduced a fee waiver task force focusing on tracking and reporting fee waivers. The result? Fee waivers went down more than 50%, resulting in a bottom-line improvement exceeding $5 million.

Conclusion

With non-interest income potentially approaching 50% of total revenue, most banks are woefully under-skilled in sophisticated pricing for fees. Increasing business judgment founded on a meaningful fact base will be pivotal for banks' achievement of revenue targets going forward. This, in most cases, can only be achieved either as a dedicated review process or as part of undertaking a more comprehensive change program.

Understanding perceived customer value of the products and services offered is not a trivial or easy task. Elasticity grids, regular market benchmarking and evaluation of pricing initiatives are a few of the tools that are increasingly becoming best practice for the market leaders in the industry. And although the revenue management sophistication applied in other industries is a very remote target for most banks today, it will become industry practice over the next decade as the battle for customers' fees continues.

"Focusing on customer value and examining price elasticity opened our eyes to significant revenue opportunities at Signet."

Malcolm S. McDonald

Former Chairman and Chief Executive Officer

T. Gaylon Layfield III

Former President and Chief Operating Officer

Signet Bank

Richmond, Virginia

Elasticity: The Forgotten Component of Pricing

Banks have more pricing flexibility than they think

Originally published in Bankers Magazine July/August 1988

Reprinted with permission

Financial institutions have significant scope to improve their pricing strategy for personal financial services. Indeed, most institutions could improve their net profits by 10 percent to 20 percent on implementing a systematic approach to pricing. Contributing to the repricing latitude available to financial institutions are wide differences in customer price elasticity (the ratio of the percentage change in demand caused by a percentage change in price) — a component in the pricing equation that is not well known to many financial institutions and therefore unexploited by them.

One trait that sets the personal financial services industry apart from other industries is that, by and large, it has a limited understanding of what its customers really value, and its customers, though inured by years of regulation to standard and undifferentiated products, do have their preferences. Catering to these preferences and adjusting features, real or perceived, to satisfy different market segments' needs could allow financial institutions to differentiate prices and maximize profits.

Why are the concepts of value to the customer and customer price elasticity insufficiently understood in the financial services industry? The reasons are mainly historical. When heavily regulated, financial institutions had little incentive to understand their customers. When deregulation came, understanding costs and service profitability became important, but only recently has a handful of institutions begun to study customers' price elasticity in a rigorous and systematic way.

It is not that financial institutions attach little importance to price setting — quite the contrary. What is surprising is the gut-feel, seat-of-the-pants approach that seems to be the rule. In fact, financial institutions pay a heavy penalty in forgone profit for their lack of pricing sophistication. This article reviews current pricing methods and the toll they exact and presents an improved, systematic approach to pricing for financial institutions.

Prevailing pricing methods

In the old days, suppliers had little need to develop expertise in setting prices for personal financial services. The government regulated them and everything else as well — products, services, industry practices, and ranges of allowed activities. Cross-subsidization flourished, and there was little room to understand costs or margins. Spreads were generous — even inefficient players could earn good margins.

When deregulation broke this cocoon and forced institutions to set their own prices, two methods became popular: cost-based pricing and competitive-based pricing. Neither is adequate. Both result in sub-optimal pricing; both cause the industry to lose profit opportunities.

Cost-based pricing

The price formula in cost-based pricing is cost plus margin, which means that a company must know what its costs are. After deregulation, many financial institutions had neither records of their costs nor knowledge of them. So, a good number of these organizations embarked on the painstaking task of finding out how much it cost them to sell and service their products. The efforts went on for years, using the standard unit-costing methods of manufacturing companies.

However, although cost information is crucial for many business decisions, it is not of great value in setting prices for two reasons.

First, financial institutions have a high proportion of shared costs (i.e., costs that are jointly incurred by a group of products and services) and many ways of allocating them to arrive at the base cost. For example, the costs that retail bank product share — branches, computer systems, statements, and many other items — often exceed 50 percent of total costs. The allocation methods are almost as numerous: they include floor space, revenues, number of transactions, managerial time, and dozens more. In allocating the shared costs to products and services, institutions realize that results can differ dramatically with each allocation method they use. Since they are not sure which method is best, knowledge of costs does not help them select the "right" price list.

A second argument against cost-based pricing is that it ignores customer price elasticity and thus fails to optimize price. In many cases, financial institutions that are making a profit on a small percentage of their customers are unwilling to raise the prices for unprofitable customers, since most of them cover their variable costs and help to carry the overhead. Although there is a good deal of truth in this argument, excessive dependence on cost analysis in price setting can mean forgone profits. If customer research indicates that customers are not price sensitive, institutions can raise prices and increase their profits by as much as 20 percent.

Despite its serious shortcomings as a sole determinant of price, thorough knowledge of cost has its place in the price-setting process. It enables institutions to see which price levels are sustainable in view of the existing competitive price structure. Knowledge of costs is, therefore, a necessary, but not sufficient, condition in a proper pricing process.

Competitive-based pricing

Knowledge of competitor prices is valuable in the same way. Often, however, financial institutions rely on the market or major competitors to set the "right" price levels. Competition-based pricing has two major drawbacks: (1) a price follower frequently adopts the price without giving much thought as to whether a company's cost structure can support that price; and (2) again, customer price elasticity is not considered.

At times, competition-based prices can be advantageous if a price leader is maintaining a price umbrella at levels that give most institutions comfortable margins, and high entry barriers prevent invasion by new entrants. However, price leaders usually do not know any better than followers what constitutes the right price and, in some financial sectors such as property and casualty insurance, competition-based pricing has had extremely adverse effects (the so-called insurance cycle).

Like knowledge of costs, competitive analysis has its place in the pricing game. It helps an institution to put things in perspective to answer the following questions:

- Are our prices in line with our competitors?

- Can we make a profit at prevailing prices?

- Are the market prices an indication of the industry's cost structure?

- If so, are we the low-cost or high-cost producer?

An improved approach

The limitations of current pricing practices, coupled with forgone profits, suggest the need for a new approach to pricing, one that starts with customers' behavior and only then factors in cost and competitive considerations. To move toward this integrated approach, financial institutions must first understand price elasticity better than they do now. They can then trace the implications of this understanding through the pricing system and build the requisite capabilities.

Understanding price elasticity

Financial institutions, even those known for their marketing orientation, rarely try to understand the price elasticity of their customers. Price elasticity is a function of many factors — most typically, amount of payment, frequency of purchase, complexity of product, pricing structure, switching costs, availability of information, and image. Not all of these factors come into play in every case, and, of course, other factors can also enter into a particular situation.

The first step in the elasticity analysis is to pinpoint the factors to which customers are sensitive in buying different financial services and the level of response those factors trigger. In the following section, this article will examine four of these factors by way of illustration: (1) amount of payment; (2) complexity of product; (3) switching cost; and (4) image.

Amount of payment

As a rule, the higher the amount of payment, the higher the price elasticity. Mortgage payments are an example of high consumer price elasticity — customers react strongly to even small changes in rates. Because the monthly payments often amount to 20 percent or 30 percent of a consumers' take home pay, mortgage holders hurry to refinance their debt even at a small rate decline.

Credit cards, on the other hand, are a good example of low consumer price elasticity — customers are nearly indifferent to price levels. This is because monthly payments are typically small, usually ranging around $20 to $40 per month.

Indeed, the behavior of credit card holders has puzzled economists. Every year, card holders spend larger amounts of money and incur greater debt. This phenomenon occurred at a period when card interest rates hit record highs while issuers' funding costs declined significantly.

Consumer advocates have complained loudly about greedy financial institutions, but card holders' low price sensitivity has endured. Confirming this persistence are the historical experiences of two smaller banks that pioneered lower credit card rates. Bank and Trust of Connecticut lowered its rate by 5 percent and managed to attract only approximately 50,000 new customers. Only about one-third of these customers switched from other banks, lured by low rates.

A small California bank — Central Bank of Walnut Creek — had an even more discouraging experience. After lowering its credit card rate by 2 percent and conducting an extensive marketing campaign, it increased its cardholder base by 11.5 percent. Revenues stayed flat, however. Any increase due to the growth of the cardholder was offset by the decline of interest revenue. Disillusioned after a few months, the bank sold its entire credit card portfolio to another institution.

Complexity of the product

The more complicated the financial service, the lower the price elasticity. Life insurance products are a case in point. The calculation of real returns on policies entails advanced financial analysis beyond the capabilities of most consumers. In fact, the many payment options and investment alternatives are so overwhelming that even some insurance agents admit that they do not fully understand how the products work.

Insurance buyers who rely on agents for explanations are in most cases so bewildered that they buy whatever the agents recommend, and agents, more often than not, have a vested interest in recommending certain policies. In all, the product complexity and agents' lack of objectivity work in the same direction. Consumers buy life insurance policies with little regard to price.

Switching costs

When switching costs are high, consumers are less price elastic. Checking accounts are a good example of a product with a high switching cost and relatively low price elasticity. It is expensive in terms of check costs and inconvenient in terms of time required to switch to another bank. It should hardly be surprising that cheaper accounts often go begging while customers stick to their higher priced accounts.

Image

Few financial products have succeeded in differentiating themselves through the use of image. Premium credit cards, however, are the exception — the difference between premium cards and regular cards is mainly one of image. Premium credit cards connote an exclusive and upscale image — the incremental benefits to which premium card holders are entitled, are, for the most part, insubstantial. These benefits often include luggage tags, luggage retrieval service, credit line, more travel insurance than the regular card, and so on. How many credit card holders would actually purchase these auxiliary services if given a choice?

The incremental costs related to different types of credit cards—especially advertising and exclusive benefits — are unlikely to add more than 5 to 10 percent to the providers fixed costs (i.e., costs unrelated to usage intensity). Although costs are only slightly higher, annual fees for premium cards can be more than 100 percent higher than the annual fees for regular cards. In essence, the high annual fees, considerably in excess of the economic value of the card, buy an upscale image, and higher price is itself part of the perceived benefit of the product.

Implications for banks

This examination of four of the factors affecting consumer price elasticity highlights how important it is for financial institutions to understand their customers when pricing their services. The opportunities—and implications—are far reaching:

1. In insisting on the commodity-like nature of the majority of their products and services, financial institutions have been taking an excessively gloomy view of their pricing flexibility. They should recognize that consumer price elasticity exists, they can change a number of factors that influence price elasticity, and they have plenty of room to maneuver. It is

up to the financial institution to use these various levers in the most effective way — to increase profits while providing each customer with the best price-to-benefit ratio.

2. Customer analysis should be the first element of a three-pronged pricing analysis, ahead of cost analysis and competitor analysis. For customer analysis, institutions need research skills. One research capability that is immediately useful in selecting the best price levels is "trade-off" or "conjoint" analysis. In conjoint analysis, consumers are asked to make trade-offs among the features of certain products and services, and each trade-off is quantitatively linked to price. For example, for a new checking account product, the features under consideration may include interest rate on balances (0 percent, 1 percent, 2 percent); transaction charges (no charges, $0.10, $0.25); Online Billpay (no privileges, complete privileges); minimum balance ($500, $1,000, $2,000); and so forth. Consumers are shown cards or respond to computer screens displaying different combinations of features and are asked to rank them in order of preference. By sorting cards, consumers are making a value judgment about each of the features, including the price they are willing to pay.

3. Once they understand the different price elasticities of customers, financial institutions can segment customers and tailor their services to the needs of each group. Such customer segmentation benefits both parties: consumers' needs are better met, and providers can optimize their marketing and pricing strategies.

The final ingredient for sound price setting is building pricing capabilities: the ability to develop a good company strategy and design product strategies; the skills to analyze customer behavior, costs, and competitive behavior; and, finally, the ability to select and implement the appropriate product or service pricing strategy.

All these elements make up a systematic approach to pricing, and financial institutions need to make sure that they are following such a strategy.

Conclusion

The pricing approaches financial institutions have been using since deregulation are woefully inadequate — and worse yet, they are taking their toll on forgone profit opportunities. Institutions should exploit the unique latitude they have to leverage their customers' price elasticity through creative and differentiated pricing. Our research with clients estimates that understanding customer value/price elasticity and using it to adjust prices can improve profits by 10 to 20 percent — and in some cases even more. The systematic pricing approach described in this article lays the road to such improvement.

Reprice Products to Reflect Value and Risk

Originally published in American Banker May 19, 1994 (Part 1 of 3)

Reprinted with permission

Banks have failed to understand the true nature of their complex cost structures, and have seriously underpriced their products and services to reflect the value they provide, geographic differences in relative price sensitivity, and the specific risk of commercial borrowers. Banks need to systematically reprice their product lines to reflect value and risk.

Moreover, banks attempting to adjust the inadequate pricing of the past must now battle both consumer advocate groups and antitrust regulators, who will make repricing in the future even more difficult.

Corrective formula

An approach that focuses on customers' perceived value and risk profiles can help correct past errors in pricing and lead to a 15% to 20% increase in a bank's non-interest income with negligible, if any, account run-off.

This is the first of a series of three articles on how banks can approach the necessary redesign. We will present the reasons for the underpricing phenomenon and its impact in this first part, then move on to a technical foundation for a better understanding of pricing, and, in part three, show how to link price to value.

Simply put, bankers often do not know how to price. But they have the opportunity, with repricing, to increase pretax income by $10 billion to $15 billion annually. Capitalizing on this potential should be one of the top priorities for CEOs.

Historically, bankers had little need to develop expertise in setting prices for transactions, which has resulted in a general lack of pricing sophistication. Interest rate regulation provided a subsidy that made it unnecessary to understand the specific value customers placed on individual services and transactions.

Products were bundled for pricing purposes, services were cross-subsidized, and it was not important to understand costs, margins, or relative geographic and borrower risk differentials.

With deregulation, institutions were forced to set their own prices. Cost-based pricing and competition-based pricing became popular. Both were inward-looking approaches that resulting in gross mispricing.

Faulty methods

The formula used in cost-based pricing is cost plus margin, which obviously means that a bank must first know what its costs are. The fact is that most banks don't have a true understanding.

While many have embarked on the painstaking task of allocating costs to producers and customers, they have used the standard unit costing methods of manufacturing companies (which is essentially meaningless in banks) to allocate the common costs of shared branch networks, back-office processing, and so on.

Knowledge of competitors' prices is a valuable but insufficient element of optimal pricing. Price leaders often do not know any better than followers what constitutes the right price in terms of value.

Value-based pricing

The limitations of current pricing practices should be contrasted with value-based pricing, which is rooted in customer behavior, and only then factors in cost and competition. Such an approach focuses explicitly on customer price elasticity (i.e., the percent change in demand for every percent increase in price) at the transactional level.

Relative sensitivity to price is a function of many financial and psychological factors, most typically: amount of payment, frequency of purchase, complexity of product, pricing structure, switching cost, availability of information, and image.

Market research provides compelling evidence that customers value bank services far more than bankers think. In a recent *American Banker* survey, consumers ranked price as the seventh-most-important factor in dealing with a bank.

One indication of customer loyalty is that almost 50% of "mom and pop" businesses have been with their primary bank for 10 years, or more. Among consumers, that number jumps to more than 60%. Three out of four small business customers and 66% of individuals are "very satisfied" with their bank.

Reaction to price changes

But the true test comes when actually raising prices. If the bank does so beyond the value that customers attach to its products, they will simply take the business elsewhere. Prices can be selectively raised, however, provided products and services are unbundled, and reviewed based on perceived customer value instead of cost-plus pricing.

Figure: Shifting Consumer Surplus to Bank Surplus by Applying Value-Based Pricing

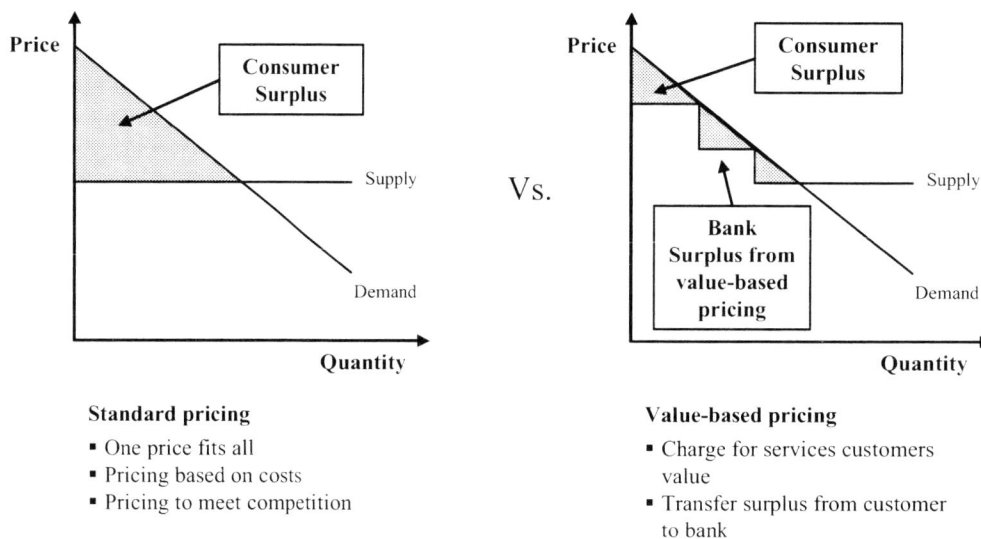

Standard pricing
- One price fits all
- Pricing based on costs
- Pricing to meet competition

Value-based pricing
- Charge for services customers value
- Transfer surplus from customer to bank

This is not restricted to markets where competition is scarce. Even when customers have the option of switching institutions, banks can increase their transaction revenues by 15% to 20% simply by adopting selective repricing based on customer value — with less than 1% run-off concentrated in very-low-balance accounts. This amounts to $8 to $10 billion in forgone pre-tax earnings for the industry.

This is not to suggest that a thorough knowledge of costs — at least direct costs — and competitor prices has no place in the price-setting process. It enables institutions to see what price levels are unsustainable in view of existing capacity and current competitor prices.

Customers' perceived value however, should be the dominant driver of pricing.

Geographic differences

Banks have also seriously underpriced transaction services and interest margins to reflect geographic differences in price sensitivity. They have begun to address this issue largely as a result if industry consolidation.

Recent Federal Reserve studies have found that, as bank mergers cause power to be concentrated in fewer hands (particularly in states like California, where the market is already more concentrated than elsewhere), customers tend to earn lower interest rates on deposits.

And borrowers, particularly small businesses, are charged higher rates for loans. This does not imply, however, as consumer advocates charge, that there is cause for concern that "the little guy will pay" for consolidation.

Underpricing by weak thrifts

Deposit and lending yields that vary geographically are most often a reflection of past irrational pricing by weak savings institutions, not price gauging. From the customers' perspective, competitors are rewarded for having both a higher share of distribution locations and the right type of distribution (such as branches or ATMs) in the right place. In short, location is everything.

The pricing potential of concentration — provided it does not overstep the bounds of antitrust constraints — is both significant and justified by customers' behavioral preferences. A rough estimate of the potential of such price differentiation is as high as $4 billion pretax annually for U.S. banks. Yet many banks have failed to capitalize on this potential for local pricing.

Borrower risk pricing

Finally, banks have failed to price effectively for their true cost of lending, once the relative risk of borrowers is taken into account. This is especially true in commercial lending because of the changes in demand and supply factors during the 1980s.

Commercial loan demand has decreased because capital market alternatives such as commercial paper, medium-term notes, junk bonds, and derivatives have provided more efficient and less expensive options or all but the riskiest borrowers. Meanwhile, alternative suppliers such as foreign banks, insurance companies, and finance companies have made significant inroads into the market. The result is overcapacity without rationalization.

Banks have simply been underpricing for the commercial loan risk — often essentially equity risk — that they have assumed. Such underpricing costs the U.S. banking industry roughly $2 billion a year pretax.

* * *

To fix their past failings, banks must do the following:

- **Price to value.** Since transactions and services have a definable and quantifiable value to customers, bankers must refrain from cost-based charges or competitor-matching prices, and follow consumer product marketing standards of value pricing.

- **Price geographically.** Understand that customers will pay more for local convenience. Customers are not irrational in failing to arbitrage geographic price differences; they understand the forgone income or cost, but trade it off against what they value more highly.

- **Price loans for differential risk.** Bankers must break down the respective risks of different borrower segments (just as investment bankers do with mortgage-backed securities or insurance companies do with pools of car insurance risks) to differentiate their loan pricing. If banks cannot be the engine of recovery from the "credit crunch," there are alternatives available, such as middle-market and small-business loan securitization, which can provide companies with financing while giving a fair return to investors.

- **Lobby for rational pricing.** A significant educational process is required to illustrate the justification for future repricing to allow price and value to be brought back to equilibrium.

Study of Products and Their Perceived Value Can Point Way to Acceptable Price Increases

Originally published in American Banker June 2, 1994 (Part 2 of 3)

Reprinted with permission

A necessary starting point for getting beyond the pricing mistakes of the past is to unbundle the full range of products and services offered by each business into their component parts.

Automated teller machine services, for example, might be broken down into withdrawals, deposits, balance and account inquiries, fund transfers and "off-us" transactions that generate surcharges.

Then, the revenues associated with each business area's product or subproduct components can be determined, establishing a starting point for evaluating repricing potential.

Bankers often do not price products at the subproduct level. Even when they do, there is usually little data available for quantifying the associated total revenues of each.

Therefore, total revenues for a product are disaggregated to each subproduct based on transaction volumes, allowing the bank to observe the overall demand for products and services at the component level and to examine the "reasonableness" of current pricing.

The bank's direct cost of offering subproducts establishes the absolute minimum price it can charge without losing money. Since many banks have no true understanding of their costs, however, scores of products and services are offered at low prices, below what is needed to cover variable costs, let alone contribute to fixed costs.

The following analyses are designed to enable the bank to approach repricing armed with the cost information necessary for evaluating options:

- ***Product workflow.*** To identify all of the costs associated with the delivery of specific products and services, a work flow chart that details the major tasks involved with each process is prepared. Just as unbundling allows banks to view products and services in terms of their component parts, the work flow chart illustrates the various activities associated with providing each subproduct.

- ***Unit costs and the cost/price comparison.*** This involves deriving the total cost associated with the subproduct's activities, then comparing the unit cost of the product as a whole to the price per unit currently charged.

Using ATM services as an example, one bank found that the total controllable annual cost of the processing component was $2.9 million. With five million transactions per year, this translated into a processing cost per unit of 57 cents. When the costs of the other components were added to processing, the cost per transaction equaled $1.40. A comparison of this unit cost with the current price per unit of 25 cents on a bundled basis helped set future ATM fees at the subproduct level.

- **_Customer relationship analysis._** This requires the identification of those customers who contribute the most to cost and profit, first by estimating the revenues associated with specific customer segments and then by comparing those revenues with the associated transaction volumes and costs they generate by subproduct. The goal is to detect any imbalance between the level of tailored services provided to specific customer groups and the revenues obtained from them.

Analyzing the economies of its corporate trust employee benefit plan customers, one bank discovered that less than 8% of customers, representing over 77% of total assets for the product, produced 43% of total revenues and just 8% of the costs.

At the same time, 71% of customers, holding 7% of total assets, produced only 27% of total revenues and 80% of costs.

Perceived value

Understanding the "perceived customer value" of product components is the crucial link between cost, current revenues, and repricing potential.

To achieve a broader understanding of perceived value, it is necessary to measure how much importance customers attach to each of a product's main attributes, compare the bank's ability to meet the needs of its customers with that of its main competitors, and examine the relationship between price and value for each product.

This analysis provides a foundation for assessing the "price band positioning" of the bank's products and services (that is, the bank's prices relative to competitors for the respective value they provide), and allows the identification of situations where the value of specific products exceeds the price charge. The following steps are taken to achieve this objective:

- ***Identifying and ranking product attributes.*** From a customer's perspective, attributes are defined as the specific needs fulfilled by each product. Once the attributes of a product or service have been identified, the next step is to rank each attribute in terms of its relative importance to the bank's customers.

To provide a basis for comparison, the same ranking is carried out for each of the bank's main competitors using available market and product information.

- ***Determining surplus value potential.*** The bank is now prepared to compare its ability to meet customer needs with its competitors' ability to do so, and thereby to examine the relationship of between the value that customers attach to products and the prices that are currently charged. Thus, the potential for repricing specific products, services, and transactions can be identified.

For example, one bank discovered that it was offering an estate planning product at a substantially lower price than its key competitors. Raising prices to realign charges for its product's relative value increased revenues by more than $700,000.

The last step in preparing for the evaluation of repricing options is to review the bank's relative market share over time, versus historical price changes and competitor responses.

Bankers are often concerned that a variety of price increases will have a severe impact on their current account balance and transaction levels.

To allay this fear and help establish the available latitude for price increases, customer price sensitivity is analyzed. Data are gathered showing the precise amount of each price change by product in the past, competitor responses, and the resulting impact on the number of accounts and net revenues.

Historical pattern emerges

This establishes any historical patterns of run-off, and, in most cases, illustrates the rarity with which historical price changes have affected revenues — typically less that 1% for price increases of even 20%.

Thus, revenue contribution analysis at the subproduct level creates the context for examining the reasonableness of current pricing; a careful review of products and services based on perceived customer value and surplus value potential sets the stage for generating repricing opportunities; and market analysis provides the competitive parameters within which repricing can occur.

The preparatory steps described above involve painstaking, detailed analyses of the bank's current patterns of pricing.

Laying a foundation

Understanding current pricing, however, simply forms the backdrop for the generation of repricing options that specifically link price to value and focus explicitly on customer price elasticity at the transactional level.

Such analyses need discipline and structure if they are to be carried out effectively, but they are an indispensable foundation for the comprehensive and creative approach to bank transaction pricing that will be discussed in the final article of this series.

Repricing Product Lines Can Bring Big Returns

Originally published in American Banker June 9, 2004 (Part 3 of 3)

Reprinted with permission

Banks need to reprice their product lines systematically to reflect the value of those products to the customer and the cost to the bank.

The results of systematic repricing are impressive — for example, $16.3 million in additional revenue for Star Banc (now U.S. Bancorp) and $43 million for Bank of Hawaii, constituting a 19.4% and 20.1% increase, respectively, in fee revenue.

Our previous two articles showed why banks have mispriced in the past, and provided the analytical foundation for a new way of thinking about pricing. In this article, a comprehensive and creative approach to reappraising banks' pricing will be outlined.

Linking price to value provides the core foundation for generating repricing options. It provides a basic framework for comprehensively reappraising the bank's prices at the subproduct level. However, under the value umbrella, several dominant repricing themes emerge: namely, streamlining product and service offerings, charging for the value of tailored service, standardizing and simplifying product delivery, tiering prices, and identifying new pricing opportunities.

Streamlining Offerings. By streamlining product and service offerings, banks are able to reduce the number of overlapping products and eliminate products and services with low customer usage. Not only does this reduce the level of customer confusion, but also substantially improves the overall profitability of individual product lines.

One bank, for example, discovered that its branches still supplied more than 100 distinct deposit account products—grandfathered from multiple earlier acquisitions—to very specific categories of customers. Streamlining these accounts increased revenues by $3 million annually.

Charging for Value. In charging for perceived value, the objective is to match the fees charged for each of the bank's products and services to the relative value attached to them by the bank's customers.

In situations where the customer attaches high value to a particular service, providing a more tailored approach may be warranted (where the bank's unique brand of service and superior ability to meet the needs of customers, for example, contribute greatly to its market position, or enable it to retain its most valued customers).

Analyzing the relationship between the price charged and the value customers attached to each of the bank's products, and comparing this with competitors, allows the identification of areas with repricing potential.

What Do Rivals Do?

To illustrate, the perceived customer value of one bank's business premium savings product exceeded that of its four key competitors, while the price charged to customers trailed three of the four. The bank used this information as the basis for increasing the price charged for the product to the level of its competitors. This generated $400,000 in additional revenues.

In situations where the customer perceived value is believed to be low, the option of raising prices in order to dissuade customer use should be seriously considered.

For example, one bank offered a purchase protection plan as an enhancement to its credit card product simply because this was available with competitors' cards. The bank discovered, however, that the perceived customer value of its purchase protection plan was low. This allowed the bank to raise the annual fee charged for the plan and thereby reduce the number of subscribers to the point where service could be completely eliminated. The policy change had no impact at all on the overall number of credit card holders.

Standardizing, Simplifying. Customer relationship analysis identifies the revenues generated from specific customer segments and their associated transaction volumes and costs. It reveals the extraordinary amount of embedded cost that exists in tailoring products and services to the specific needs of individual customer groups. Standardizing transactions and simplifying product delivery, by limiting the degree of tailoring, can materially reduce these costs.

As an example, most banks have by now come to realize that publishing one central customer service phone number, rather than each individual branch's, ensured that customers received a consistent level of service quality, while reducing the cost of such service.

Figure: Standardizing and Simplifying Products

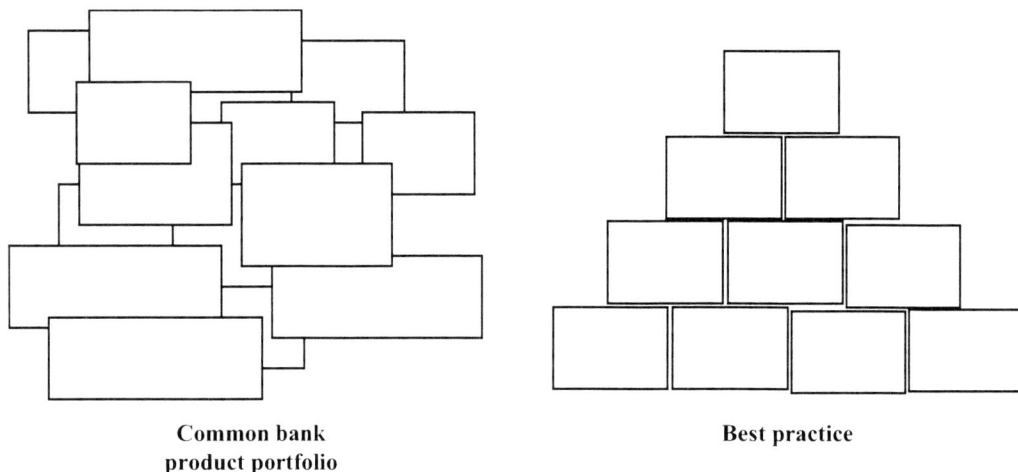

Common bank
product portfolio

Best practice

Examining costs in this way can increase the bank's pricing flexibility to lower charges for the rationalized product or service offering.

Tiering Prices. Information gathered through the customer relationship analysis also helps to identify which customers contribute the most to cost and profit, enabling the bank to reprice products and services to reflect the size of customer balances or volumes of transactions — that is, price tiering.

Those customers having the highest balances and lowest transaction volumes often contribute the least to the bank's overall cost.

Charging more to customers with lower balances and higher transaction volumes can therefore enhance the revenue and profitability of product lines without risking the loss of the bank's most valuable customers. To achieve its full potential, this form of differential pricing should be applied to the individual components of each product to help ensure that the price ultimately charged reflects the actual costs of low balance/ high volume users.

At one bank, tiering prices on its consumer liability products led to $2.2 million in additional revenues. Changes included introducing low-balance fees on certain demand deposit accounts with balances less than $200, establishing a pin-based POS-transaction fee on accounts with balances less than threshold levels and implementing a $5 low-balance maintenance fee on personal money market savings accounts, among other charges.

Figure: Typical Profitability Distribution of Checking Accounts

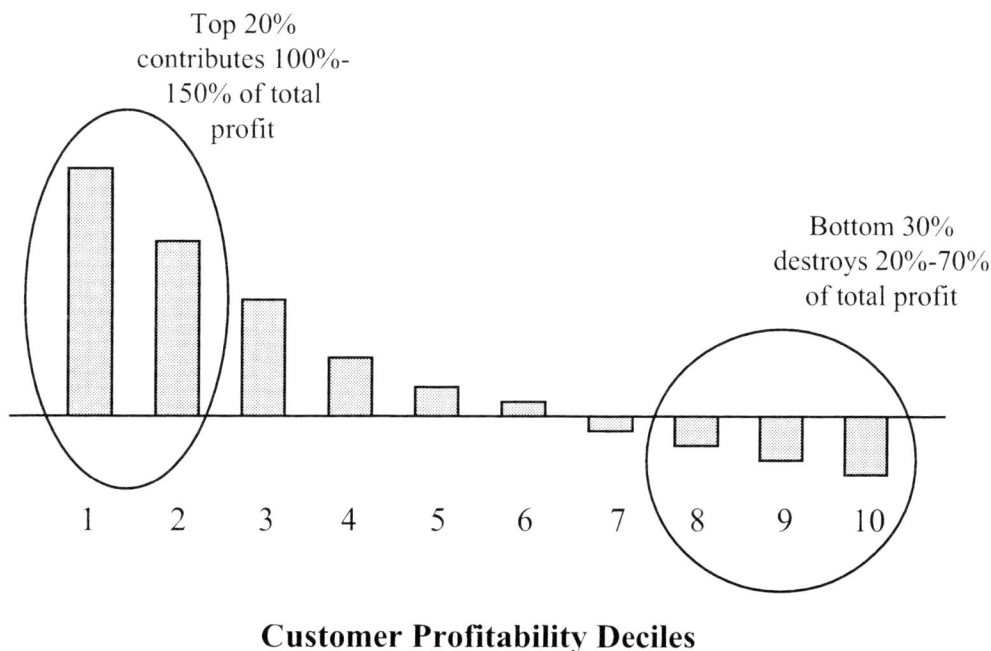

Top 20% contributes 100%-150% of total profit

Bottom 30% destroys 20%-70% of total profit

1   2   3   4   5   6   7   8   9   10

Customer Profitability Deciles

In exploring new pricing opportunities, the bank designs new products that can be delivered by leveraging its existing resources. Doing so offers each business area a fresh source of revenue, and helps to enhance the overall profitability of specific product lines. Since there will be very little, if any, basis for pricing these products initially, the bank should approach such pricing conservatively until an adequate amount of information can be gathered to evaluate the level of each product's success.

For example, at negligible incremental cost, one bank began offering a money market fund to outside mutual funds that did not have a product of their own. Upon obtaining just one new account, the bank increased its revenues by $400,000.

The final key issue when exploring repricing is how to address the inordinate amount of the bank's revenues lost annually to fee waivers. Limiting the number of occasions that customers are relieved of their obligation to pay fees allows the bank to eliminate the chronic abuse of escape clauses for specific groups of customers.

One bank discovered that these waivers amounted to over $4 million in lost revenues out of a total potential of about $80 million. Hardwiring fees and only selectively granting waivers reduced lost revenues to under $1 million.

The above broad-based themes collectively provide a basic framework for addressing the value and cost issues uncovered by the analyses outlined in our second article.

Based on the specific characteristics of each business area, a portfolio of repricing ideas, centered around these themes, can be developed consisting of as many as 500-750 individual repricing opportunities.

Two further steps, however, are then required:

- ***Run-Off Analysis.*** Employing the results obtained by analyzing the run-off caused by historical price changes, the bank is able to quantify the likely run-off and net revenue impact of each proposed repricing idea, and the portfolios collectively. The expected reduction in number of accounts, account balances, transaction volumes, and the resulting net revenue impact at various price points, helps set the overall boundaries and risk profiles for the proposed repricing options.

- ***Burden Analysis.*** This establishes the degree to which individual customer segments are affected by the combined impact of the proposed repricing ideas. Calculating the relative resulting change in fee burden and overall contribution for each customer segment across all product lines prevents the bank's most valuable customers from bearing a disproportionate share of the proposed repricing. In situations where such customers would bear too high a burden, the bank revises the repricing proposals accordingly.

Discipline in pricing to generate recurring streams of fee income is critical to meeting the ongoing earnings challenge. The repricing potential is there; capitalizing on it should be one of the top priorities on bank CEOs' agendas.

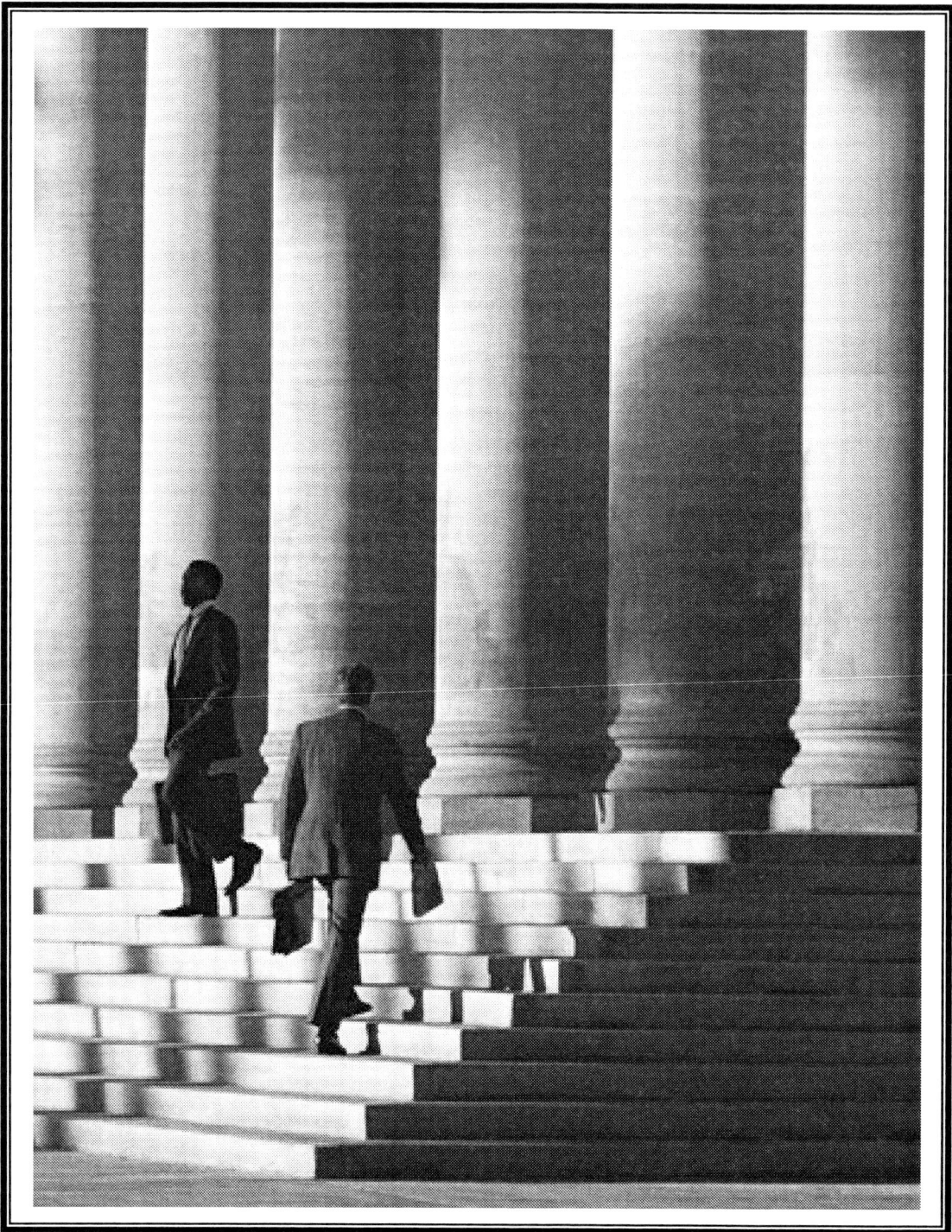

MANAGING FOR EFFECTIVENESS

Chapter 5 Introduction

Managing for effectiveness focuses on the process of redesign and doing better things as opposed to doing the same things at lower costs. While this concept has had many different "brands" over the years (reengineering, BPR, CPR, six sigma and total quality management along with dozens of others), the core challenge remains how to organize and conduct day-to-day business optimally. When we first published "Reengineering the Bank" in 1994 and "Creating the New Bank" in 1996, we could not imagine the level of response they would generate.

Ten years later, a recent headline in *American Banker* read: "Running Theme Continues – Redesign." The article discussed efforts to operate more effectively at National City, M&T, PNC, and Huntington, demonstrating that the frameworks we invented fifteen years earlier continue to serve as key strategic themes in the industry.

This chapter starts with the ideas that have impacted the modern history of banking so fundamentally. Originally published as a two-part series in 1995, these two articles helped define the industry we know today ("The Challenge of Redesign: Banks Can't Afford to Ignore It" and "Process Redesign Can Put the Industry's House in Order") and set the stage for our later work.

We firmly believe that corporate cost cutting as an effective management strategy in its own right has little sustained value. Customer-focused business process design on the other hand is the foundation for sustained, superior performance. Done right, it is a catalyst for organizational culture change, enhanced customer satisfaction and significant shareholder value generation. Done wrong, it stultifies growth.

Costs can only be cut once, and often lead to greater revenue loss in the longer term. Customer-focused design has significant economic impact, but continues to provide annuity value to shareholders.

Redesign Case Study

STRATEGIC DRIVERS GUIDE DESIGN: OPTIMIZE RISK BASED PRICING   *ILLUSTRATIVE*

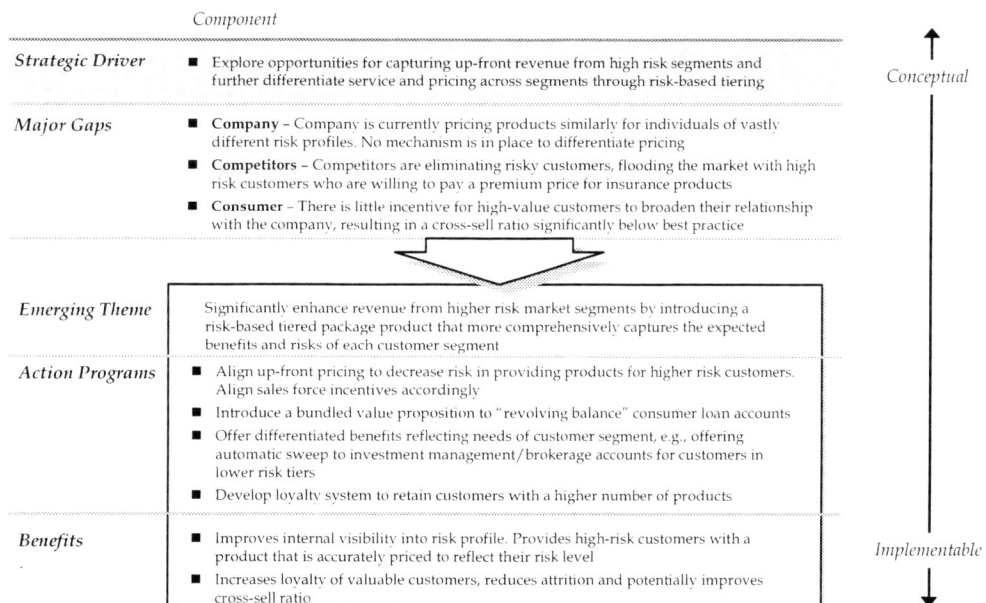

	Component	
Strategic Driver	■ Explore opportunities for capturing up-front revenue from high risk segments and further differentiate service and pricing across segments through risk-based tiering	*Conceptual* ↑
Major Gaps	■ **Company** – Company is currently pricing products similarly for individuals of vastly different risk profiles. No mechanism is in place to differentiate pricing ■ **Competitors** – Competitors are eliminating risky customers, flooding the market with high risk customers who are willing to pay a premium price for insurance products ■ **Consumer** – There is little incentive for high-value customers to broaden their relationship with the company, resulting in a cross-sell ratio significantly below best practice	
Emerging Theme	Significantly enhance revenue from higher risk market segments by introducing a risk-based tiered package product that more comprehensively captures the expected benefits and risks of each customer segment	
Action Programs	■ Align up-front pricing to decrease risk in providing products for higher risk customers. Align sales force incentives accordingly ■ Introduce a bundled value proposition to "revolving balance" consumer loan accounts ■ Offer differentiated benefits reflecting needs of customer segment, e.g., offering automatic sweep to investment management/brokerage accounts for customers in lower risk tiers ■ Develop loyalty system to retain customers with a higher number of products	
Benefits	■ Improves internal visibility into risk profile. Provides high-risk customers with a product that is accurately priced to reflect their risk level ■ Increases loyalty of valuable customers, reduces attrition and potentially improves cross-sell ratio	*Implementable* ↓

"Aston drives an engaging and inclusive program that is uniquely tailored to each organization's specific needs."

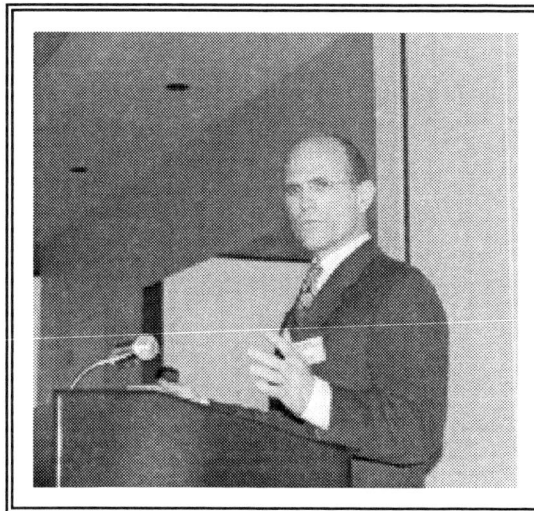

Tom Hollister

Vice Chairman

Citizens Financial

Boston, Massachusetts

The Challenge of Redesign: Banks Can't Afford to Ignore It

Article originally published in American Banker
August 9, 1995

Reprinted with permission

Salomon Brothers interviewed more than 50 leading banks in 11 major markets to evaluate the industry's success in controlling costs and to determine how performance might be improved. The survey concluded: "Cost management has become a dominant strategic theme throughout the banking world...The major lesson from the handful of successful, low-cost producers is that a cultural commitment to cost management, invariably driven forcefully throughout the organization by the chief executive, is the single most important success factor...If this culture is in place, the techniques of successful cost management are proven...[and] are summarized under the heading 'redesign.'" A decade later, this theme still resonates as a strategic priority in the industry.

I would add that true redesign looks at both sides of the income statement; re-pricing of services based on the "perceived" value banks supply to customers is comparable in importance to successful future competition. Bankers must therefore acknowledge an imperative to redesign. This may seem a surprising assertion, given the industry's record earnings of the last fifteen years. Yet redundant and dated cost structures, unsophisticated pricing models, and the convergence of competition with non-bank suppliers are collectively leading to an earnings crunch for banks that the industry must meet head-on.

Senior and middle-ranking bank managers face an enormous cost challenge. By its nature, the banking business involves an inherently more complex structure of process, functional, physical plant, and systems costs that are common to multiple customers, products, and geographies.

In response to niche marketing by product specialists, banks have introduced a flurry of "new" products and services. Although some of these efforts have helped retain a departing customer base, many have a "flavor of the month" quality. This latter characteristic creates a three-fold effect: first, the dilemma of whether to create a specialist product sales force and infrastructure; second, the need for increased cross-selling by marketers and even tellers; and third, the further burdening of systems and operations to serve the increasing number of products and services.

If costs were complex for the core bank, further complication has arisen from the industry's continuing consolidation. The number of banks has declined from over fifteen thousand to less than nine thousand in the past fifteen years. Bankers hoped that geographic expansion would give them access to more customers, thereby leveraging their product mix and allowing them to achieve economies of scale on the cost side. Bank mergers, however, have added the challenge of managing geographically remote affiliates.

In a valiant effort to cope with their complex cost structures, bank investment in information technology now exceeds $30 billion per year and appears to be steadily increasing after the dotcom bubble. This investment may be warranted by the needs to upgrade to meet capacity constraints, make improvements required for customer ease of access and speed of turnaround, and avert competitive obsolescence vis-à-vis peers. Yet it is far from clear that these investments have achieved the projected cost displacements that were their justification. And the increased value of service to customers through such upgrading has not been reflected in increased prices.

All of this has led to a burden on the management structure of banks through matrix management, narrow reporting spans, and successive layers of process "controls" that have made banks incredibly inward-focused.

The results of a general lack of pricing sophistication are evident across all product lines within the banking industry. Most pricing models used today are still based upon cost-plus or competitor matching approaches, both of which focus inwardly rather than reach out toward the customer.

The limitations of traditional pricing approaches should be contrasted with value-based pricing, which is rooted in customer behavior and, only then, factors in cost and competitive factors. Such a model focuses explicitly on customer-price elasticity — that is, the percent change in demand for every 1% increase in price — at the transaction level.

The failure to manage process costs and process effectively is more significant because of the fierce competitive challenges banks now face. This is true on both the consumer and commercial side of the bank.

In consumer banking, on the liability side, banks have lost a significant source of low-cost funds, as consumers have shifted their deposit balances to CDs (in favorable rate environments) and are increasingly more comfortable investing in mutual funds and ETFs, annuities, and other investment options.

Though deposit disintermediation has raised the cost to banks of doing business, non-bank product specialists have also "cherry-picked" the most profitable retail credit niches. From the mid eighties through the late nineties, commercial banks' market share among the top 25 credit card issuers fell consistently as Capital One, MBNA, Providian and other specialists gained significant market share (only to have banks re-acquire that share through acquisitions, e.g., Bank of America's purchase of MBNA and WAMU's purchase of Providian).

In commercial banking, the increasing sophistication of markets and corporations has prompted development of cheaper alternatives to traditional bank financing. The maturing, and consequent liquidity, of the commercial paper market turned short-term financing into a commodity-type product, based solely upon the issuer's credit rating. This has given corporations an efficient means of funding that banks often can not match given their inherent cost structure. To illustrate, from 1980 to 2005, corporate commercial paper borrowings grew from $124 billion to $1,646 billion.

Even the weakest credits have been able to obtain non-bank sources of long-term financing — primarily through the high-yield or junk bond market.

Total Yearly High-Yield Corporate Bond Issuance and Commercial Paper Outstandings
1990-2005 ($ Billions)

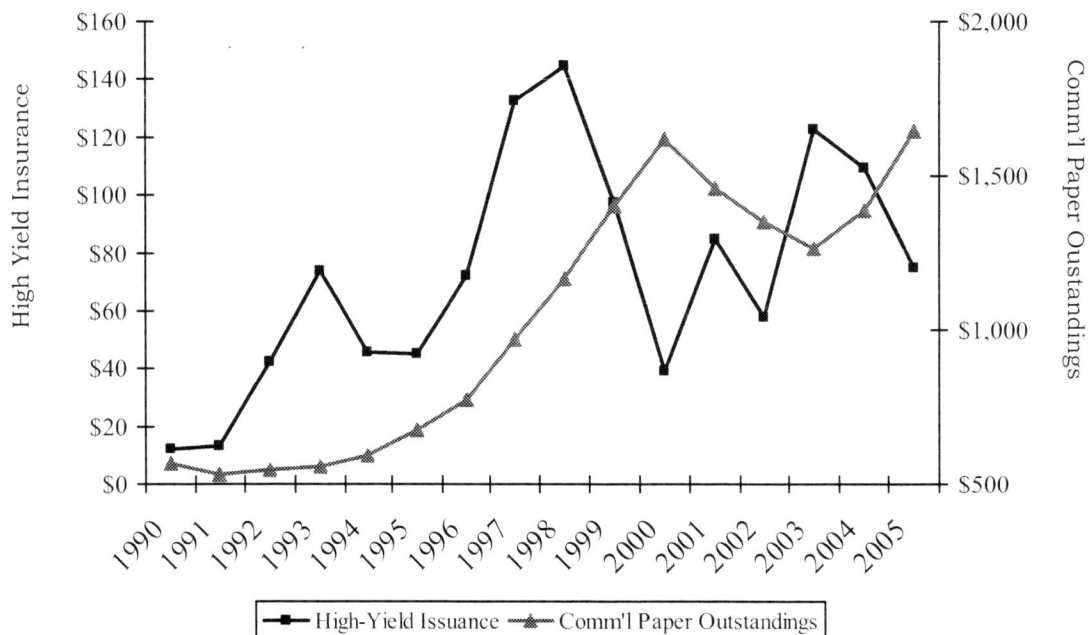

Source: Federal Reserve

Product specialists, national competitors, and increasingly sophisticated customers are creating a competitive environment in which only efficient producers and banks with sophisticated pricing practices — banks or non-banks — will survive.

The margin of error for underperformance is continually narrowing. Yet bank costs are almost always too high and their prices too low.

The average cost to income ratio for publicly traded banks continues to be about 63%. However, top quartile performers are operating with cost to income ratios of 40% to 45%.

In the past, regulation and limited competition prevented the development of a discipline that would inspire bankers to challenge arcane, redundant, or duplicative processes — at an enormous cost. Pricing has, at best, been on a cost-plus or competitor-matching basis. Industry-wide, the earnings left on the table from this imbalance of costs and pricing are of the order of $30 billion a year, before tax.

And hungry, fierce competitors are waiting at the door to capitalize on banks' economic vulnerabilities.

Redesign: Can Put the Industry's House in Order

Article originally published in American Banker on
August 16, 1995

Reprinted with permission

Redesign is acknowledging that the way things have been done in the past is not sacrosanct, and that a new competitive environment and new technologies require radical new ways of doing things. In institutions both large and small we have seen the reinvigoration of staff and corporate culture once employees are empowered to look at the bank from a "blank sheet of paper" perspective.

Redesign focuses on the only significant, controllable lever that can be used to manage bank costs: redesigning the web of interlocking processes that drive them. Processes are sets of inputs that create an output of value to the customer. Tasks, on the other hand, are the numerous, discrete activities that fulfill demands of each process. Redesign operates at the process level, in order to design the organization to do better things, rather than doing the same things in a better way or at a lower cost.

Moreover, a true redesign examines all of the bank's processes. Retooling individual processes or functions does not work in banks, given the interdependencies among the various functional, process, physical plant, and systems cost levers and across the strategic, organizational and management layers of customer, product, and geography.

Many "restructuring" programs focus, instead, on individual processes or tasks. This causes them to be performed more cost efficiently (at least in the short term), but does nothing to challenge the underlying assumptions of the interlocking processes within banks that generate these costs.

When a comprehensive approach is taken to redesign, however, the organization ends up streamlined from a cost perspective but, more importantly, better disciplined in credit decision-making, more customer service-oriented, and culturally refocused outward to its market and competitors.

Redesign requires the systematic design of the bank's cost processes, driven from both the top down and the bottom up.

REDESIGN IDENTIFIES THE DRIVERS FOR CHANGE IN A TOP DOWN-DRIVEN, COLLABORATIVE FASHION...

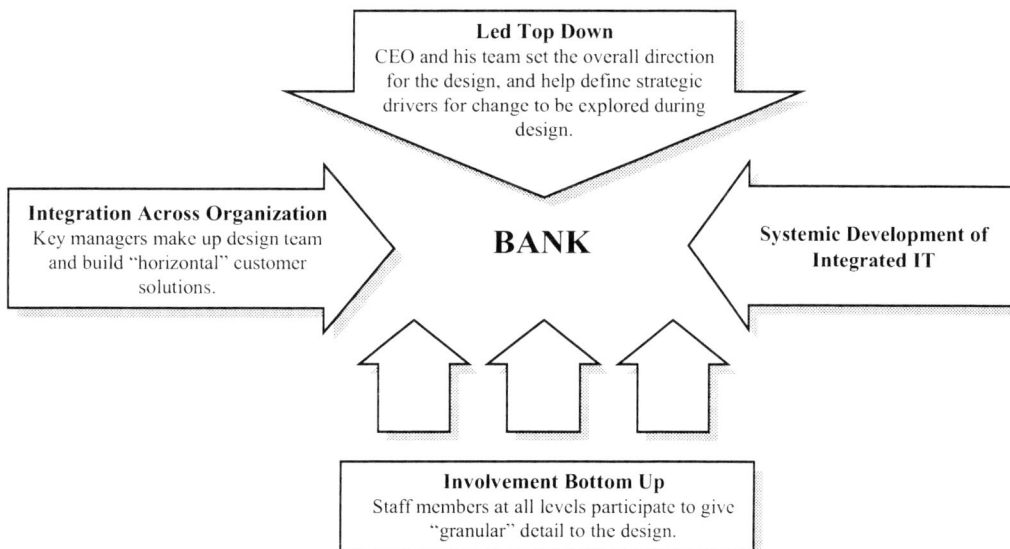

Led Top Down
CEO and his team set the overall direction for the design, and help define strategic drivers for change to be explored during design.

Integration Across Organization
Key managers make up design team and build "horizontal" customer solutions.

BANK

Systemic Development of Integrated IT

Involvement Bottom Up
Staff members at all levels participate to give "granular" detail to the design.

The top down approach requires the senior management of the bank to identify basic, structural redesign ideas for each area on the cost side — branches, retail credit, wholesale, trust, systems, operations, and administration — to evaluate.

The bottom up element draws upon all of the resources and staff of the organization, as employees brainstorm ways to remove redundancies and inefficiencies from their day-to-day activities.

Branch redesign ideas. A structural theme within the branch network is to provide more of a customer orientation by removing back-office-type processing and administrative activities from the branches, which commonly account for over half to two-thirds of branch staff time.

Branch efficiency ideas. Efficiency ideas generally allow employees to take more responsibility for their functions and remove supervisory layers that "control" the interaction between the staff and customers. Although, individually, they may not generate tremendous financial gains, in the aggregate they instill a new customer-oriented culture that yields significant results.

Thus, redesign is not arbitrary, across-the-board cost cutting, as it is often disguised euphemisms like "restructuring," "total quality control," "downsizing," or "horizontal management." Arbitrary programs simply do not work.

Nor does redesign always result in staff reductions in all areas. Costs in banks are dominated by personnel expenses. Fundamental economic redesign, therefore, does often result in substantially lower employee numbers. Such reduction is selective, however, reflecting the relative value-added of the processes served by each position.

When a redesign approach is perceived as an effort to create a truly new bank — and not a knee-jerk "fire drill" to meet unexpected earnings downturns — employees become enthusiastic and involved.

The potential impact of redesign on process costs. As a result of banks' efforts to expand geographically and technologically, while increasing product offerings, operating costs per bank employee in the United States have increased 86% from 1990 to 2004. Clearly, if this trend continues, it will be difficult for banks to compete in the increasingly specialized markets.

Redesign will revamp a bank's cost structure by getting to the root of the problem. Since costs ideally do not "creep back," business process design produces an annuity impact to earnings. For the industry as a whole, the potential is roughly $30 billion, or over 20% of estimated 2004 pretax earnings.

The impact on the bank culture. When the chief executive officers of banks who initiated such programs were asked to describe the top five results of a bank business process design program, the most frequent responses included:

- Significantly improved customer service;

- A reinvigorated corporate culture focused on sales;

- A de-layered management structure, with senior managers closer to customers;

- A new economic profile with an efficiency ratio of between 40 to 45%; and,

- Significantly improved stock price, up between 30% and 50% within six months of the completion of the redesign.

The goals of business process design are to create an institution with superior customer service, with a focus on profitable sales opportunities, and with a culture of "can do," not "can't do because..."

If properly structured, and led by committed senior management, these objectives are achievable, and also fundamentally enhance economics through sustainable, recurring earnings.

REDESIGN CALLS FOR BROAD ORGANIZATIONAL EVALUATION OF POTENTIAL OPTIONS...

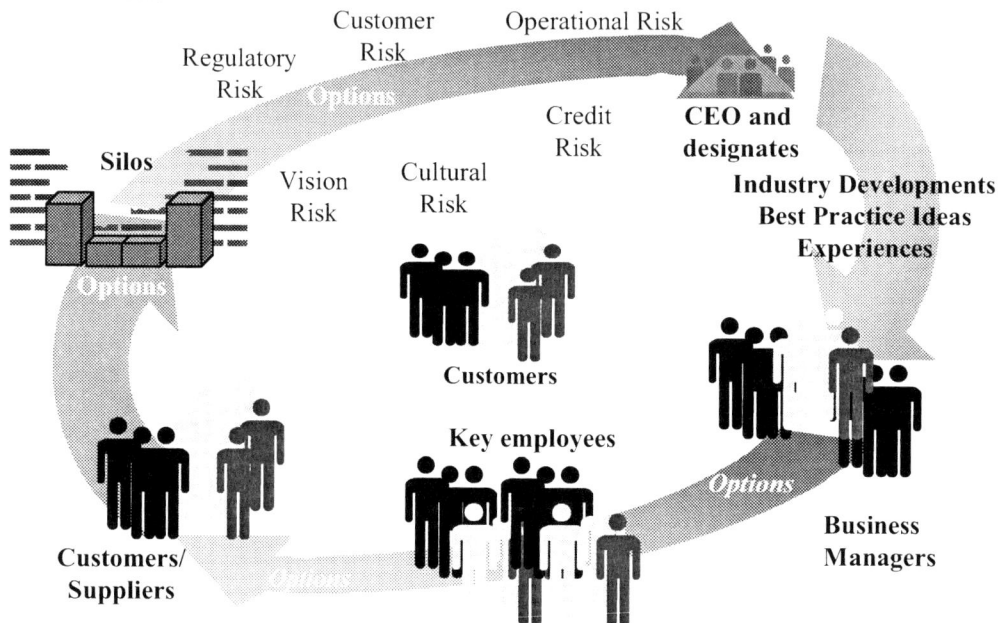

Implications for the industry's future. With the Gramm-Leach-Bliley Act being enacted in 1999, some of the pessimism of many banking pundits — not to mention bankers themselves — dissipated as the perceived uneven playing field was leveled. A period of prolonged earnings growth, superior credit quality, as well as general optimism was followed by a wave of mergers that brought together banks, investment banks, insurance companies, and niche product providers such as credit card companies. However, the underlying economics of the banking business did not change and the reality of increased competition, narrowing spreads, challenges in containing costs and growing fee income remained. In the aftershocks of 9/11 and the accounting scandals that led to the adoption of SOX 404, cost complexity continued to mount.

While bankers continue to enjoy many competitive advantages on which to capitalize, including a unique distribution network of branches, automated teller machines, and internet platforms; a loyal, highly trained sales force; sophisticated transaction processing; securities and foreign exchange trading technologies and skills; and, most important, the exceptional loyalty and inertia of consumers, small business owners, and the like, the mandate for change remains.

This is not a matter of incrementalism. It is not a case of minor fixes to marginally improve efficiency due to the same old things of the past at a slightly lower cost. Banks need to radically redesign their basic processes and business approaches to reflect the realities of competition. They must continually reinvent themselves. And examples of successful business process design prove that this is not wishful thinking. CEOs with the vision and courage to face the economic realities of their industry are empowering their staff to redesign the bank.

They are using the resulting improvements in stock value to fund acquisitions, and then capitalizing on the discipline instilled throughout the bank as a result of business process design to realize consolidation benefits so often lost in the past.

They are tackling the new entrant intruders head on and they are winning. True redesign is not easy. It involves challenging each precept of traditional banking and remolding an institution's culture.

Yet if structured and managed as outlined, it can be an exciting and reinvigorating experience that binds the institution — whether large or small — more tightly together, while returning its focus to customer sales and service.

Banks can continue to enjoy the earnings growth of the past 15 years and beyond. They can meet and overcome the challenges they face. To do so, however, they must step up to the plate and confront the business process design imperative now.

Fundamental Changes Needed to Ward Off Revenue Crunch

Article originally published in American Banker on
March 10, 1994

Reprinted with permission

The banking industry has enjoyed its recent run of benign external factors: solid economic growth, a robust housing sector, historically low levels of loan losses and positive returns and subsequent growth in the equity markets.

Demand, Pricing factors

Yet, if new demand for bank products — most importantly loans — does not materialize, the industry will be faced with a revenue crunch. The crunch comes from both demand and pricing factors. On the retail side, the demand for bank products and services has been significantly affected by continued pressure from non-banks including insurance companies, asset managers and mono-line card players.

The current flat yield curve, expectations of loan losses normalizing and the real estate sector cooling are three factors adding strain to banks' expectations for future revenue growth.

Capital Market Options

In the commercial sector, the evolution (and resulting liquidity) of markets for such products as commercial paper, medium term notes, and high-yield bonds — along with the advent of derivatives and securitization to diversify the risk of these products — left banks with a much smaller, and riskier, range of companies to which to lend. As demand has shrunk, loan under-pricing has become prevalent. Banks have failed to price for borrowers' risk or have simply misunderstood their own cost structures. Loan Pricing Corp., New York, has estimated that a small-business borrower, with a rating B-minus, would have to pay nearly 250 basis points over the cost of funds to cover historical losses. In fact, the average yield has been between 300 and 350 basis points, leaving only 50 to 100 basis points to cover marketing, credit administration, and branch servicing costs, and to provide a contribution to overhead — not to mention a return to shareholders.

Trading Revenues

Earnings generated by the bank as principal (primarily foreign exchange trading profits and securities gains and losses) have been greatly enhanced recently, aided by strong performing equity markets. According to FDIC data, aggregate commercial bank securities gains reached all time highs of $6 billion in 2002 and 2003, while retreating to $4 billion in 2004. Maintaining such record-high levels going forward cannot be guaranteed.

Credit Quality

The emerging revenue crunch has in fact elicited varying responses from the industry. While another wave of credit losses has yet to materialize, there are troubling signs suggesting that recent history could repeat itself. In the early

1990s, the effects of the "credit risk binge" nearly had catastrophic consequences for the industry resulting from banks seeking to offset high costs with higher-yielding loans. Today, we know that the increased margins did not compensate for the additional risk, and resulted in write-offs of almost $110 billion between 1990 and 1992.

Flavor of the Month

Increasing the number of products and services offered to customers — most spectacularly, the consistent focus on financial advice and product extensions like mutual funds — has enabled some banks to cope with a deteriorating core business. However, for others, "flavor of the month" specials have contributed significantly to increased operating costs, yet have had only a marginal impact on customer retention. In fact, the issue of balance cannibalization continues to challenge the industry.

Ominous Signs

The revenue crunch has serious implications for all financial institutions, but particularly for the many banks that are counting on asset growth to provide redemption from high levels of non-interest expense. While many believe they can "grow into their cost base," there are ominous signs that quite the contrary is true. Industry deposit growth has nearly stalled completely after years of solid growth and heavy investments in branch infrastructure. Similarly, growth in home equity and residential mortgage originations has slowed as concerns over a slowing real estate sector continue.

It is therefore imperative that banks seize the opportunity to preempt the revenue crunch by redesigning their cost structure to become a low-cost producer, and redesigning their pricing to reflect their customers' true price sensitivity, given the value that banks provide. Cost structures must compete effectively with the host of niche-oriented, non-bank product specialists. The average efficiency ratio (costs to revenues) for publicly traded banks, while improving, remains stubbornly in the mid-60s. Top-quartile banks, however, operate with efficiency ratios between 40% and 45%.

In our experience, most banks can reduce non-interest expenses by 15% to 20% to produce an annuity (rather than a onetime) earnings impact without endangering customer service or business strategy. This freed capital can subsequently be re-invested into higher growth areas. On the other hand, if a thorough examination of costs is not conducted, the increasing commoditization of bank products will eventually drive high-cost producers out of the market.

The possible revenue crunch won't disappear through a miraculous combination of loan growth and product expansion.

Nothing less than a fundamental redesign of bank economics will allow the industry to evade the crunch.

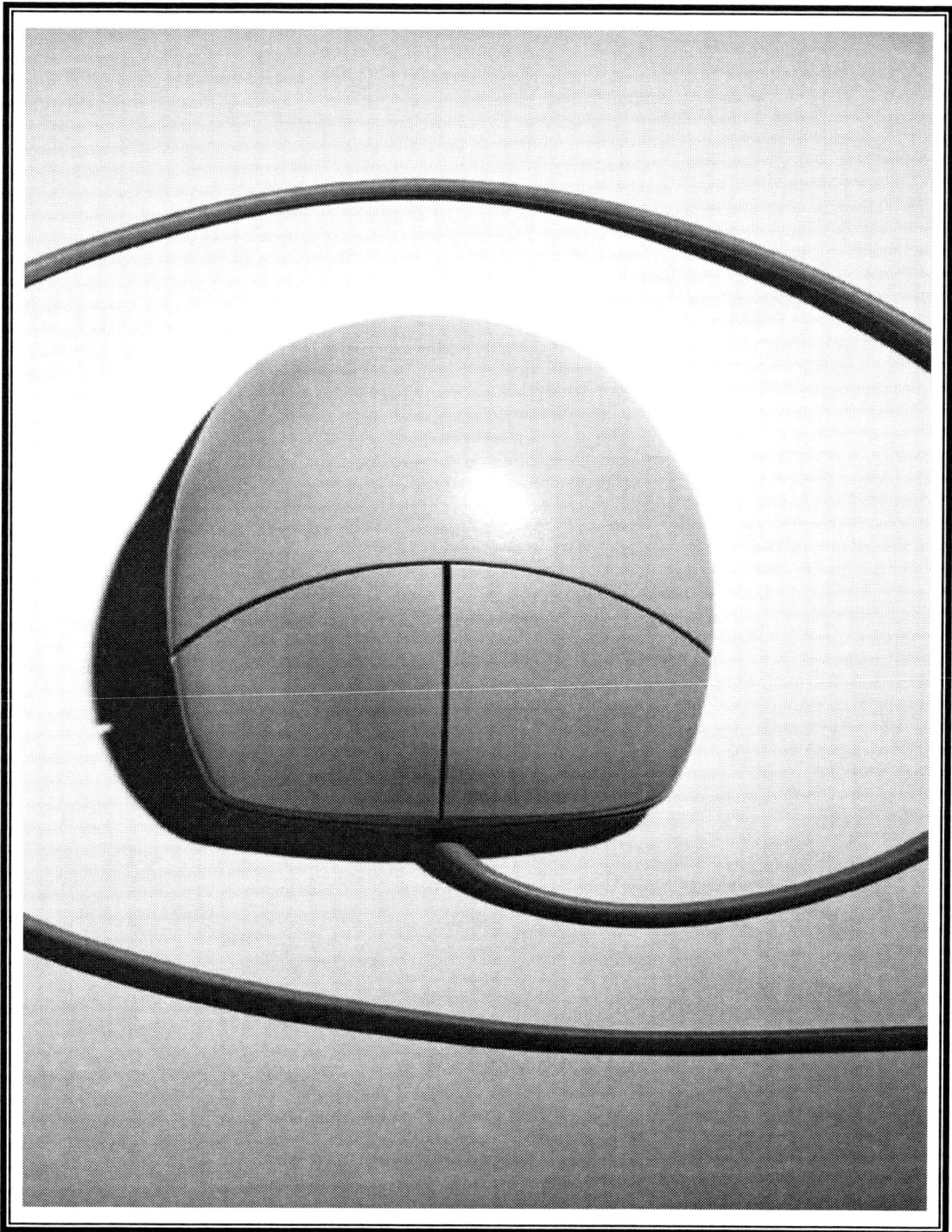

MAKING
TECHNOLOGY WORK

Chapter 6 Introduction

Information Technology is one part of banks' infrastructure where a revolution has taken place on our watch. From stodgy mainframes, via early PCs, to web-based, object-oriented front- and back-office solutions, the tools available to banks have developed continually. To what extent bank CIOs have taken advantage of such tools has, of course, varied. Add the challenges of Y2K, Sarbanes-Oxley and Internet security, and the world of bank IT has been everything but uninteresting over the past fifteen years. The added layers of complexity, from increased functionality to systems integration to security demands, have made banking the lead industry in terms of IT budget as a percent of total revenue.

IT Budget as a Percent of Revenue by Sector (2009)

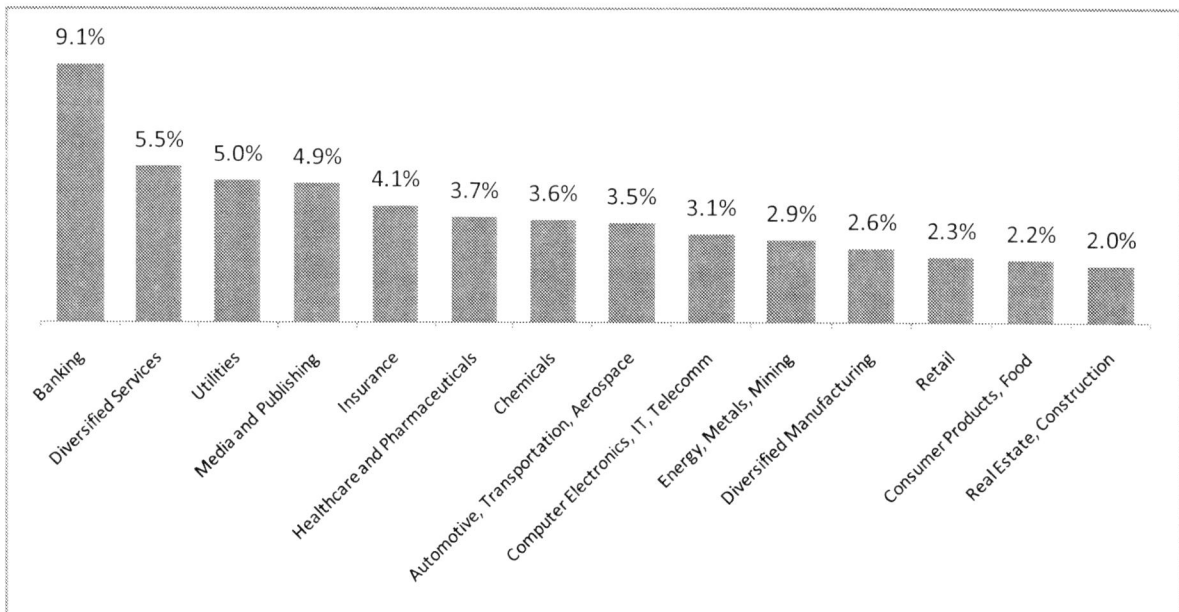

Source: Corporate Executive Board

While technology continues its pell-mell development, the focus of financial services technology has begun to shift. While huge amounts of money are still being spent on IT, more and more of this is moving from providing the latest technology to partnering with individual business units to ensure that IT dollars are being spent effectively and that business unit priorities are understood and provided for.

Relative Focus of IT Strategy for 2008

Average Allocation by CIOs of 100 "Pennies" Across Areas of Strategic Focus

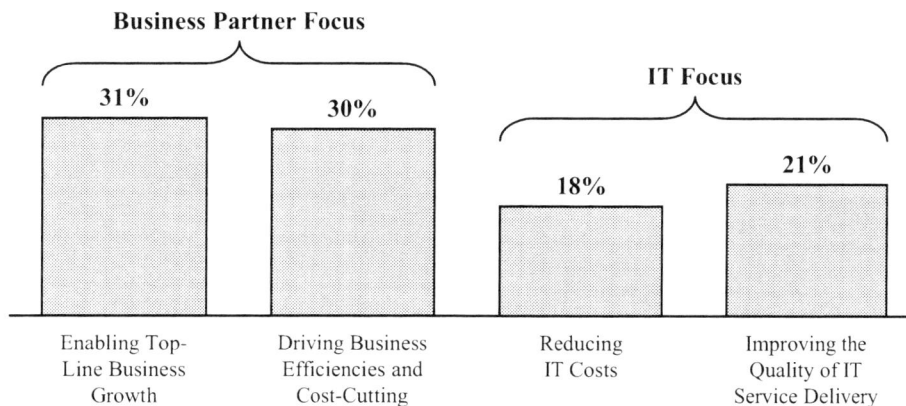

Business Partner Focus   **IT Focus**

31%	30%	18%	21%
Enabling Top-Line Business Growth	Driving Business Efficiencies and Cost-Cutting	Reducing IT Costs	Improving the Quality of IT Service Delivery

"Managing the Transition to New Bank Technology" analyzes the various core system challenges and opportunities banks face. The article explores different methodologies for redesigning IT systems and processes. While some of the systems discussed are no longer the latest available, the concept of comprehensive process redesign remains as true today as it was at the time of the article.

"Value Added Outsourcing for Transition Management," originally published in 1995, was clearly ahead of its time, with outsourcing and off-shoring becoming part of everyday language by 2006. The recommendation of outsourcing the most appropriate functions, rather than simply the most functions, is particularly apt as overall outsourcing spending has begun to

Source: CIO Executive Board, "IT Spending and Budget Benchmarking Results," 2008

flatten and even decline in recent years (outsourcing represented 13.4% of total IT budgets in 2006, 13.1% in 2007 and was estimated at 12.7% in 2008).

Finally, in "Note to CIO: Launch an Incremental Value Performance Index (IVPI) for IT to Demonstrate Value to Businesses," our team examines how appropriately to align IT support with overall business strategies, and ensure that IT projects are prioritized based on business needs.

"*We were convinced that the energy and drive unleashed through our partnership with Aston Associates was one of the crucial factors in the success of our efforts.*"

Bill Balderston, III

Chairman and Chief Executive Officer (Ret.)

Chase-Lincoln First Bank

Rochester, New York

Managing the Transition to New Bank Technology

Originally appeared in American Banker July 10, 1995

Reprinted with permission

Many bankers assume that taking advantage of the benefits of modern technology means first improving economies of scale, but this need not be the case.

Financial institutions have a viable alternative to striving to get bigger.

Those that want to improve their technological performance can do so by harnessing the practical and proven applications of client/server technology, and by using selective outsourcing of applications development, processing, and network management to cover skills gaps during transition.

This transition from legacy-based mainframe systems to the "brave new world" of technology can be achieved either through incremental change or through comprehensive redesign.

Most if not all banks will attempt this transition. Their success will depend on how well it is managed.

Economies of Scale?

Most bank chief executives come face to face each year with a daunting bill from their data center and network operations management.

This bill is always in the multi-million-dollar range, yet a good portion of it is not for new technologies; it is for the development and maintenance of legacy systems.

Of the $2.1 billion spent on bank technology in 1995 exclusive of large-scale outsourcing and service bureau costs, $1 billion went for that purpose, Tower Group estimates.

These vast sums are being spent on processing data on mainframes, and developing and maintaining legacy systems. Such systems are designed to handle a large volume of transactions. They are driven by economies of scale.

The demands for large-scale processing have increased in recent years, as the pressure for product differentiation has driven banks to add complex functionality to their legacy systems to support alternative delivery channels.

These legacy systems, designed for simple accounting transactions, require a lot of hardware and network resources in order to accommodate the demands of alternative delivery. The programming procedures required to deliver higher functionality, and to circumvent the lack of relational data bases, add to processing costs.

As the complexity of legacy systems increases, so do testing needs. Since most code in legacy systems was written with little structured analysis, adding layers of functionality requires extensive testing as the only way to maintain and assure quality.

Emerging Alternative

A combination of client/server technology — which essentially calls for data to be stored, processed, and accessed where it is most cost-effective — and strategic outsourcing of selected applications development, processing, and mid-level management functions, can provide the tools for transition from the world of scale-dependent legacy systems.

The architectural design of a new bank-wide system should include:

- Moving to vanilla core application systems to support deposits processing, loans accounting and the general ledger.

- Outsourcing the development and maintenance of most core application systems.

- Developing and implementing a clear retail and commercial delivery strategy.

- Developing and implementing a data warehousing strategy to support the delivery strategy.

- Developing and implementing a client/server network to extract and process data from the data warehouse.

Effective Transition Execution

The following steps are needed to successfully implement the transition to a new technology architecture:

- Develop a specific, detailed transition plan to fit your business strategy.

- Identify and recruit the project managers and key technical specialists required to implement the transition.

- Implement the transition.

The central challenge this presents to a bank's chief executive is ensuring that the skills are in place to both develop the technology transition, and to tie these skills to the resourcing and implementation steps.

Two alternative approaches to transition are available to bank managements: incrementalism and comprehensive process redesign.

Incremental Technology Transition

In this approach, individual profit centers in each line of business drive the transition process by funding incremental projects which require aspects of client/server technology and outsourcing (through use of vendor packages). There are advantages and disadvantages to this approach:

Pros:

- In the short term, each increment in the technology transition can be cost-justified and tailored to individual profit center requirements.

- Each incremental investment in new technologies is cost-justified in supporting a specific business requirement, e.g., customer marketing and tracking databases in the trust and commercial areas each can be supported by separate and distinct solutions tailored to each profit center.

- As the incremental projects are implemented over a period of time, the bank has the opportunity to evaluate a range of vendors and gain a hands-on understanding of the evolving client/server technology.

Cons:

- In the long term, duplicative functionality and multiple data storage, processing, and network platforms will result in significantly higher costs of technology maintenance and upgrading.

- Discrete investments in "the best available" technology for specific business solutions to support individual profit centers will lead to duplication in functionality with mushrooming maintenance costs.

- The need for systems supporting individual business units to talk to each other will require the development and subsequent maintenance and administration of multiple and complex interface network applications, leading to significantly higher costs.

Comprehensive Process Redesign

This approach requires top management's total commitment and attention to the redesign process. Ideally, the redesign should include:

- A technology diagnostic to assess the current state of the bank's systems applications, hardware, and network platforms.

- A current-state assessment of each line of business.

- The identification of major technology themes to drive the transition from the current state to the future architecture.

Pros:

- The lines of business requirements drive the change in the bank's technology architecture.

- The change is built off common platforms, minimizing duplications in functionality and the need to develop and maintain complex interfaces.

Cons:

- This approach exposes the entire bank to change in a very short period of time.

Given the intensity of the redesign approach, the bank will need to have in place, early on, a technology transition team, to help the lines of business develop technology-based solutions and then use the specific business ideas as the basis for developing the new, overarching technology architecture. The technology transition team will have the following top level technology management combined with a number of specialist contracted resources:

- A top technology manager, such as the bank's chief information officer.

- Specialist technology management skills: systems architect, data base administrator, network manager, and senior project manager. (Whether these resources should be in-house or contracted will depend on the size of the institution and its current skill base.)

- Contract resources: network management, capacity management, and performance monitoring, data modeling and data management, client/server applications development, and project management.

Almost all banks are, or will over the next few years, face a technology transition. A few will address comprehensive process redesign to drive changes in technology architecture. These will end up with a strong technology team — avoiding the twin pitfalls of wasting money on legacy system Band-Aids or seeking a merger in the name of illusory technological scale economies.

Outsourcing for Transition Management

Originally published in Bankers Magazine May/June 1995

Reprinted with permission

Most current outsourcing initiatives are focused on cost reduction through transferring whole portions of a bank's operations, hardware, and systems development to a third-party vendor.

Outsourcing expertise is often occupied with finding cheaper ways to handle what banks consider commodity functions.

Little attention has been paid to adding more value to these services. With many financial institutions moving from legacy systems to those based on client/service technology, an opportunity exists for banks to get more value-added services from their outsourcing providers.

With rapid changes in technology driving down data processing costs, vendor partnerships can be created to provide value that banks cannot generate internally.

The four major challenges of value-based outsourcing are:

- Identifying areas of technology ripe for outsourcing.

- Qualifying outsourcing partners.

- Developing long-term relationships with partners.

- Creating joint ventures among partners, while managing their combined efforts.

The skills required of a bank's internal technology staff to design, structure, and manage value-based outsourcing partnerships are very different from those needed for the pure cost-focused outsourcing deals of the past.

The reward for attaining these new skills is getting a head start in obtaining tomorrow's technical capabilities.

The Cost Approach

What should be outsourced?

Traditional wisdom has been to outsource commodity functions and processes, while retaining internally the differentiating aspects of technology.

Sometimes this has translated into outsourcing the "utility," the mainframe data processing "glass house," and core operations functions.

In 1995, for example, 49% of the $3 billion that U.S. banks spent on external information technology services went toward such commodity outsourcing of data processing and related services, according to ADS/Tower Group's 1996 Survey of Information Technology Services in Banking.

The remaining expenditures for information technology service were mostly absorbed by contract programming and project management services — basically, ad hoc, project-specific "temporary help."

In this approach, the bottom-line rationale is that if an outsourcer can deliver the same service as the in-house shop but at lower cost, then the service should be outsourced. For this arrangement to be successful for the bank and the vendor, a contract commitment of at least three to five years is normally required so the upfront costs of the outsourcing conversion can be fully recovered and net savings realized.

The implication is that the transaction volumes and functionality the bank requires and the technology that can provide such service will remain relatively static.

In the last 10 years, of course, this underlying assumption has often proved wrong. However, it is this cost-based paradigm for outsourcing that most bankers and outsourcers think of when the term is used.

Adding Value

An alternative approach is to identify how significantly more value can be added by selectively incorporating outsourcing as one component in a comprehensive technology transition strategy.

In this approach, value in information technology is defined as continuing increases in the efficiency and effectiveness of services delivered to banks' customers through substantial improvements in systems development and maintenance, data processing, storage, and communication.

Such increased effectiveness and efficiency affect not only technology operations, but also technology development tools. However, the skills required to develop systems using the new tools are rapidly changing; most banks lack those skills.

Banks traditionally have taken the approach of not using any new technology until it has been proven elsewhere.

This approach is still valid. The cycle of time to prove a technology application, however, has shortened considerably.

For example, branch automation applications, which only three years ago could be evaluated and operated independently from other bank systems, now must be capable of integration with other retail applications, such as those for call centers.

Network management, client/server development, integrated development of retail and wholesale platform automation and branch automation, document imaging, and electronic check processing are other examples of areas where underlying technology processes are changing rapidly.

Yet the skill sets required to understand whether a technology is proven and then to manage the transition to absorb it into the bank are available only at a premium.

As an example: To fully leverage benefits from client/server technology, the design, implementation, and management of a cost effective data communications network infrastructure is a prerequisite.

However, the range of skill sets required to establish such an infrastructure are simply not available at most banks internally or at one vendor.

The conceptual design of the network requires technology expertise at companies like IBM or Oracle/Siebel. The follow-up physical design of the network requires input from communications engineering consulting firms independent of the major network providers. The actual implementation might be outsourced to either a major network provider (such as AT&T, MCI, or Sprint) or firms such as EDS and Comdisco, which have begun acquiring the necessary staff skills.

Post-implementation management of the network systems might be subcontracted to one of the major network providers who have the ultimate expertise in network operations.

Thus, the entire process of design, implementation, and management of the network can be selectively outsourced for discrete value-added from multiple partners, with the bank's technology managers essentially playing the role of a general contractor.

The cost of such a network, from start to completion, can be anywhere between $5 million and $20 million for a large regional bank, depending on current, but more importantly, future business requirements.

While the level of functionality to be delivered to each branch, sales, and transaction location is the basic cost driver, transforming it into a value-added program requires redesign of the underlying business processes that the technology serves.

For instance, the question of whether each branch needs a local area network server or whether clusters of branches can share one server can be answered not by the technical designers, but through the process of redesigning the basic business processes that the technology enables.

The form of such redesign will have a major impact on the costs and the value added of the network.

In the above example, the technology process being outsourced adds value to the bank by enabling a cost-effective transition away from disparate legacy network solutions to an integrated, flexible network for client/server architecture.

In such examples, outsourcing to capture value contrasts sharply to cost-conscious, commodity outsourcing.

Making It Work

For the value-added outsourcing process to be effective, the bank's internal technology organization must put in place specific frameworks, processes, and structures.

Thus, for value-added outsourcing to be effective, an overarching systems architecture blueprint needs to be in place.

The blueprint should be driven by the bank's business strategies and processes, and should form the basis for developing an overall technology transition strategy, with value-based outsourcing as one component.

The bank's information technology organization needs to develop skills to support successful, value-added outsourcing. Such skills include: continual, structured learning of technology trends and prioritization of practical transition opportunities; development of project management methodologies that allow integration of multiple vendor deliverables; and honing of sophisticated contract negotiation and contract management capabilities.

Information technology management needs to be structured to become general contractors, positioned to manage the transition toward a client/server networked architecture and away from legacy architecture and systems.

Specifically, new management approaches and responsibilities must be developed to enable information technology management to develop and sustain vendor relations, scope outsourcing programs, work with vendors in developing their proposals, evaluate and structure joint ventures between vendors, and manage the specification and subsequent adherence to service standards.

In essence, a depth of management experience in large-scale, complex partner management, purchasing, and negotiation is required.

Also, in-depth knowledge of each of the bank's line of business processes and current trends in technology to meet such needs is critical.

Structuring and staffing the information technology function to provide this form of leadership is very different from either past management of a bank's legacy systems or supervision of commodity outsourcers.

To summarize, banks can choose to use value-based outsourcing as an integral component of managing the technology transition from legacy systems to a client/server networked architecture.

To ensure the bank's success in value-based outsourcing, basic redesign of the underlying conceptual framework of its internal technology, and its processes, skills, and organizational structure are required. The payoff is a greater opportunity for success in an accelerated transition to the new world of banking technology.

Note to CIO: Launch an Incremental Value Performance Index (IVPI) for IT to Demonstrate Value to Businesses

Creating an Incremental Value Performance Index (IVPI) for information technology enables CIOs to partner with CEOs, CFOs and business leaders in more effectively planning and implementing profitable strategies. By establishing a transparent and consistent measurement tool, CIOs can better demonstrate IT's contribution to developing and implementing high value services for internal and external customers, while reducing operating costs and maintaining current service levels.

The world of bank IT continues to take on new forms and greater levels of complexity

According to a report by ABA-Tower Group, bank CIOs have been successful in moving IT expenditure to value-adding projects, while holding down maintenance costs. Despite this, large banks have experienced double-digit increases in IT spending over the last few years, while medium-sized regional banks have had expense growth of approximately 5%.

One of the ways in which maintenance costs have been managed is through outsourcing: while the largest banks have handed over 30% of their IT expenses to vendors, leading banks have moved 70% or more to external suppliers. Such major shifts to outsourcing enable cost management, while challenging competitive differentiation.

Customer service and security, employee productivity and efficient and effective project prioritization are three areas where IT will likely play a differentiating role in the near future.

The customer security challenge: The customer account security question has generated enough focus that even the Federal Reserve is concerned that it has the potential for impacting consumer confidence in the nation's banking system (besides its obvious market and legal risks for individual banks). Estimated costs of implementing customer security processes and systems are a minimum of $1 per account per year with an additional fixed cost of up to $50 per customer for hardware set up.

The employee productivity challenge: Loss of employee productivity due to online surfing during work hours has been an increasing source of concern. A recent survey by Websense / Harris Interactive shows that employees spend up to two hours on average per workday surfing the net. Striking a balance between work-related access to the web and restrictions on personal surfing, is challenging. The cost of control, including audit and monitoring systems, has to be factored into this equation. Gaining back an hour of employee productivity requires close cooperation between IT, business leaders and human resources.

The "external factors" challenge: In the last decade, CIOs have battled Y2K, the Patriot Act and the Sarbanes-Oxley regulatory requirements, as well as the opportunity created by Check 21. Managing such significant externally-driven projects, while simultaneously providing core services and meeting business needs, is a growing challenge. In order to be effective going forward, CIOs need a framework for demonstrating a project's relative value and cost to determine priority.

Demonstrating the business value of IT in an increasingly complex environment can be daunting

While many costs may have been moved to vendors to varying degrees, the approach to managing them has not changed significantly. In most banks, IT costs are managed by a budget: maintenance costs are seen as fixed, with budgeted increments, while new development decisions are made at a micro level on a project-by-project basis. As a result, there is no aggregate metric that a CFO or CEO can use to assess whether IT is operating effectively. In addition, there is no transparent metric the CIO can use to demonstrate his or her value to the organization. In our experience, such a metric should provide a reasonable answer to two questions: a) how much incremental value does IT add; and b) how much does it cost to achieve this?

To respond to the former, a CIO needs to demonstrate three things: how much incremental revenue is generated; how much lifetime customer value is created; and how much are business expenses reduced. Trying to assess all these factors on an individual IT project basis can be very difficult, if not impossible.

To respond to the latter, major operational costs need to be examined first, including costs of transactions processing (DDA, Card and Loans), EFT network, communications and item processing. Secondly, delivery channel costs (branch, online, ATM) and data mining/business intelligence costs should be reviewed. Again, assessing both direct and indirect costs of each individual IT project can be very challenging.

By including both value and cost factors in an overall Incremental Value Performance Index (IVPI), the seemingly daunting challenge of measuring IT's business value can be overcome. An effective IVPI also aligns IT with the success of the bank's overall business strategy.

Launching an Incremental Value Performance Index (IVPI) for IT to demonstrate value added

A good IVPI is built from three components: 1) revenue, 2) lifetime customer value, and 3) expense management (including effective vendor management).

Revenue: Assessing incremental revenue attributed to IT can yield surprising insights if done right. For example, one regional bank found that its fee-based revenues increased for small business loans due to an IT enhancement that allowed support of a flexible range of commitment fees. Before introducing an IVPI, only the small IT cost allocated to that enhancement was viewed as IT value added. With an IVPI in place, full benefits and total costs were included. A metric reflecting both benefits and total costs was developed to assess IVPI value. Allocation of benefits required a process analysis that identified each step required for driving revenue enhancements and specified IT components and associated costs for each process step.

Lifetime customer value: Identifying IT components in the process chain associated with retaining, deepening and acquiring customer relationships is critical when developing an IVPI. By encompassing impact on lifetime customer value, IVPI can become a strategic indicator, rather than simply a short-term, tactical gauge. In order to capture this, the impact of IT is assessed by identifying processes that touch customers and examining IT's role in supporting such processes. By evaluating what impact customers would feel if there was no IT support for these touch points, and quantifying what attrition would result, this component of IVPI indicates added value from improved customer retention.

Expense management: While incremental IT value added from business cost reduction (e.g., scanning of paper files, electronic statements, online transactions vs. manual transactions), has proven relatively easy to measure, expenses incurred as payments to external providers. Vendor management, therefore, plays a crucial role in managing unit costs for transactions, accounts and customers. Finding the balance between managing vendors' costs and achieving appropriate service levels requires constant fine-tuning. For example, moving to voice over internet protocol (VOIP) for all internal communications reduces costs, while potentially reducing service quality and increasing contingency risk. A quality IVPI factor would reflect net changes in value per dollar of internal communications cost due to the introduction of VOIP.

In conclusion, a combination of process analysis and cost-benefit discipline is used to construct a robust IVPI. By combining revenue, lifetime customer value and expense management metrics, an IVPI can become an invaluable management tool. Providing the leadership to make this a reality is a core mandate for tomorrow's successful bank CIO.

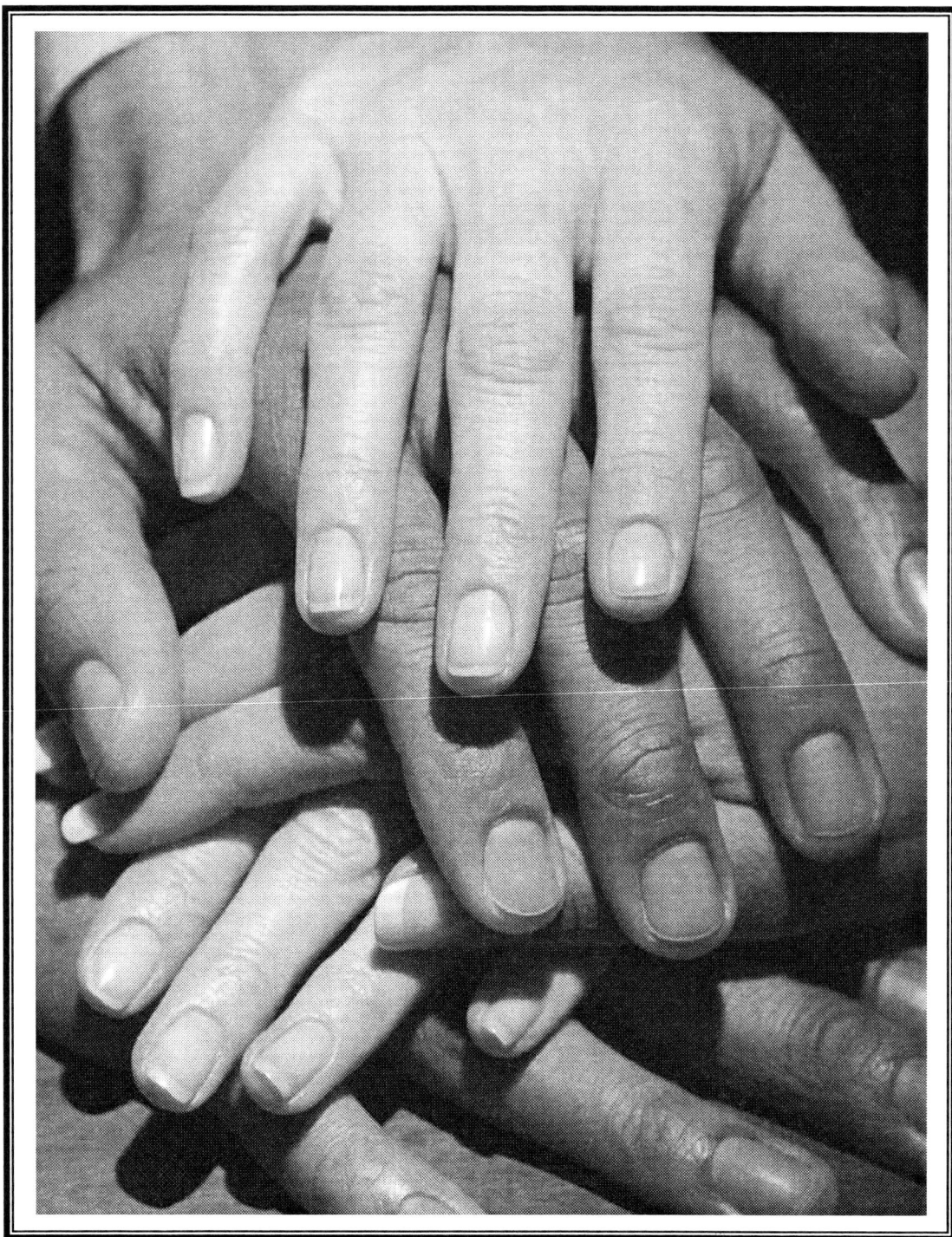

Chapter Seven

DRIVING CULTURAL CHANGE

Chapter 7 Introduction

This final chapter of published articles addresses what is surely the crux of driving lasting change and creating a performance-focused organization. Most people would agree that driving cultural change is something that takes more than an external consultant and a quick performance program. Achieving true cultural metamorphosis takes dedicated leadership, effective change strategies and – most important of all – time.

In "To Put Redesign on the Right Track Get the Staff on Board," we examine the critical importance of including your staff in all aspects of redesign in order to ensure that change becomes institutionalized.

The article "Redesign is Just a Catalyst in Culture Change" concludes our collection. Recognizing that ambiguity is the best defense for current state proponents and the worst enemy for change agents, this article concludes that ill-defined and non-specific change programs rarely achieve much. By clearly quantifying expectations, specifying time lines and obsessing with tracking results, however, a change program can become a catalyst for true cultural change. As banks look towards the next strategic horizon, nothing could be more critical.

To Put Redesign on the Right Track Get the Staff on Board

Originally published in American Banker's Management Strategies on July 10, 1995

Reprinted with permission

A recent survey of American businesses found that 85% had instituted some form of corporate redesign to improve profitability. After two years, costs had failed to decline in nearly half of those firms, and, in a few cases, they actually had risen.

The Wyatt Co. survey also found that 58% of responding companies had sought to increase productivity through "reengineering," yet only a third of those achieved this goal within two years.

While these findings were for a cross-section of American industries, our experience has been that many bank programs have a similarly limited impact.

Programs that fail are costly. In addition to the consultant's fees, there is a tremendous organizational cost. There is a huge diversion of organizational time and resources during the program. Even among employees who are not directly involved, much time is spent speculating about the latest rumors concerning potential changes.

Employee morale suffers as continual layoffs occur without any organizational revitalization. Productivity declines as workers realize that the corporate loyalty upon which they had depended has become a one-way street. Efforts to truly change the organization are performed halfheartedly, as employees adopt a "flavor of the month" attitude.

Finally, the bank and its management begin to lose credibility with its outside constituencies. Investment analysts and shareholders begin to doubt the value of the institution, as efforts to change its economics fail to deliver positive, tangible results. In the face of layoffs and closed branches, community leaders and customers begin to question the commitment of the bank to their markets.

Still, banks do have a real and pressing need for change. Most institutions have cost structures and pricing approaches that date back to an era of protection and regulation. A redesign effort forces the institution to step back and evaluate all of its processes and procedures in terms of their value to the organization.

Take, for example, U.S Bancorp. Since the bank undertook a redesign program in 1992 (as Star Banc), it has consistently outperformed peers. Since that time, its return on average assets has improved from 1.0% to 2.2%, its return on average equity has increased from 11% to 23%, and its efficiency ratio has declined from 63% to 44%.

Such growth in profitability is worth the organizational tension that redesign causes. A redesign that is properly implemented can reduce noninterest expense by between 15% and 20% and increase noninterest income between 15% and 20%.

Redesigning a bank is about organization revitalization as much as it is about redesigning cost processes, systems, and structures, or about establishing pricing discipline and outward focus. Where many redesign programs fail is in their inability to harness the organization's desire for change and channel it into creative thinking. Establishing the organizational context for redesign is as important as, if not more important than, providing a structured, managed methodology for change. Three imperatives for successful redesign must be addressed before the bank is ready to face the redesign challenge:

- Demonstrate a commitment to change.

- Demonstrate a commitment to fairness.

- Demonstrate a commitment to involvement.

Employees are much more likely to see the redesign as a permanent change in the way business is done if management truly demonstrates its commitment of the organization's time and resources.

What might be called a "layered team structure" is valuable in harnessing the efforts of the organization's "best and brightest" senior staff members, as well as employees throughout the organization.

The steering committee comprises the bank's senior executives, whose role is to set the tone for the program and lead it within the organization. This involves a considerable time commitment from them, ranging from 20% to 100% of each working day at various points during the program. The steering committee leader commits all his or her working hours to ensuring the success of the effort. A key role of the steering committee leader is to set a tone of creative thinking and radical change for the overall effort.

The team leaders include 10 to 20 senior managers who are devoted exclusively to the redesign process and are responsible for guiding it within the organization. Process leaders are responsible for analyzing current functional areas and associated processes. They generate ideas for change within a collection of cost centers or revenue growth arenas.

The third level includes all employees below the process leader level. To involve the whole staff in the redesign process, each member must be asked to contribute ideas and suggestions.

There are three advantages to this team structure. First, the direct line created between the steering committee and supervisory level mangers allows for a two-way flow of information and ideas, and thereby overcomes traditional barriers to change that result from a "bulge" of middle management in banks. Second, it takes the "best and brightest" managers away from the safety net of their line or staff positions and challenges them to think. And, it shows that senior management is dedicated to changing the way things are done.

The commitment to fairness is two-fold: fairness of approach and fairness of implementation.

To be fair, the approach must not be arbitrary. Every area and every process within the bank must be included in the redesign. If any area is excluded from review, it would be perceived as receiving special treatment no matter how valid the reason for exclusion. A commitment to fairness implies that management holds the belief that every aspect of the bank has the potential to be redesigned in a more efficient manner.

It should also be noted that across-the-board cost reduction targets or so-called benchmarking studies that mandate cost reductions without redesigning the way processes are performed are arbitrary. The true redesign of an institution requires a thoughtful review of every area of the bank, the establishment of aggressive cost and revenue targets for each, and, most importantly, a recognition of the risk associated with every idea for change. As a result, each area will be affected differently by the ultimate redesign.

In banking, it is a simple fact that staff equals cost, given the high levels of personnel expense. While some layoffs may therefore result, employee anxiety can be controlled — and staff commitment maintained — if it is felt that the redesign is something that everyone in the bank faces together and that whatever can be done to ease human resources issues will be done. This requires a detailed human resources strategy, as outlined here:

Managed hiring. At the beginning of the process it is important to limit hiring in order to provide positions for some of the employees who may be released as a result of the redesign. The bank also wants to avoid hiring anyone whose skills may not match those required by the redesigned organization.

Promotions and salary freeze. For similar reasons, promotions and salary increases should be put on hold until the process is completed. A position may undergo dramatic change as a result of the redesign and require substantially different skills than those held by the current incumbent.

Employee selection. The most fair method of selecting which employees remain with the redesigned organization is a "skills-based" assessment. Evaluate individuals against the skills required to perform the redesigned job. This method, while complex, gives the bank the opportunity to upgrade the bank's skill levels and to eliminate lower-level performers, while rewarding those employees with the most attractive sets of skills.

Severance policy. The bank's severance policies must be set in the context of the redesign effort, local employment levels, and the skills of the individuals involved. While most severance programs create a trade-off between benefits and costs, one relatively inexpensive benefit is active job search assistance by the steering committee and other senior managers to whom the individual has reported.

Re-recruitment. Human resources programs do not end with the redesign implementation. Rather, it is also critical to "re-recruit" those employees who remain with the organization. Because the displacement process may last a full year, the message that the bank is better equipped to meet the challenges of the future needs to be continually reinforced.

One of the primary reasons many redesign programs fall short of expectations is a failure to involve the whole organization in the redesign effort.

Structured and continuous communications promote a sense of participation among employees and keep all of the bank's constituencies informed about the progress and development of the redesign program.

Several steps are essential to designing a communications strategy that successfully accomplishes these goals.

Viewing the redesign program as a team effort. There should be an explicit mission statement which unifies the participants. The statement should convey the underlying economic rationale for undertaking a radical redesign. Giving a name to the redesign effort also serves as a rallying point for its supporters. The name should be simple, yet describe the project to a larger audience. Throughout the program, bi-weekly updates should keep staff informed in an honest and open fashion. Platitudes and half-truths will fool no one.

Actively directing internal communications. It is particularly important to inform key senior-level and mid-level managers early in the process and to gain the support of these leaders. Communications directed at all the bank's employees must be broad enough to give each staff member an honest and accurate overview of the program that will be carried out with in the organization, while omitting a level of detail that would generate confusion and unnecessary anxiety.

Involving external constituencies. Don't forget about the external constituencies which support the bank — including shareholders, regulators, investment analysts, the media, local communities, and the bank's customers. These constituencies should receive a consistent, coherent, and positive message concerning the redesign effort.

Involving the whole organization in what is perceived as a high priority and fair process helps create an environment in which employees believe in a process of change, participate in the way that their respective processes and activities are redesigned, and possess a sense of ownership of the changes implemented. These factors dramatically improve the ability to achieve a successful redesign of the bank which produces an annuity, rather than an ephemeral, impact on earnings.

Each of these "softer" elements of redesign is as important as, if not more important than, the specific redesign methodologies employed. Bank staff members hunger to be able to tell their families with pride how they spend their days – provided the contract is in place to seek their input, keep them informed, and use the redesign process for a one-time retooling of the bank, rather than as the latest of a series of "restructuring" fire drills.

A CEO's Perspective

We wanted to **achieve dynamic, sustainable changes** *right across the Group,* **implementing these within a one-year timeframe***, while creating real bottom line expense savings and revenue increases.*

St. George specifically **chose to avoid a cost-cutting program***. In my decades of banking I've seen many such programs. While most achieve their financial goals, they're often like starvation diets. The fat is cut, but the organization become flabby soon after because the underlying disciplines weren't there.*

Ed O'Neal
Former CEO,
St. George Bank
Sydney, Australia

The redesign program doesn't just accelerate the change process, it allows us to achieve our goals by bringing all the must-dos onto the table at once and genuinely changing our customers' experience with us*. Instead of spending multi-millions annually just to keep up with our competitors, we're spending $115 million over the next financial year and achieving four years worth of productivity gains.*

Quite simply, we believe that real shareholder value can only come from genuine customer satisfaction*, which in turn depends on empowered staff having the right tools to serve their customers.*

When we announced the result of our Best Bank organizational review, most analysts were positively surprised at the breadth and depth of our strategy.

Redesign Is Just a Catalyst in Culture Change

Originally published in Bankers Magazine's May/June 1995

Reprinted with permission

So-called "redesign" efforts often fail. Redesign is not simply headlines announcing "X slashes 3,000 jobs" or "Y will cut 20% of its work force." The immediate jump in stock price as a result of such announcements fades quickly once the negative customer and morale effects of "slash and burn" cost reduction become clear. The reason for redesign failure is that many leaders misunderstand what redesign is.

Redesign is just a catalyst (albeit a powerful and demanding one) for the long-term changes in corporate culture that all organizations must face if they are looking to serve customer needs competitively and profitably.

Old misperceptions about redesign, however, are difficult to undo; a case in point is provided by one analyst who recently criticized a redesign for taking customer and culture issues into account, as opposed to focusing purely on expense reduction. Similarly, it does not help that many consultants have done nothing more than dust off outdated cost reduction techniques and label them "redesign."

Why Does Redesign Fail?

Three recent studies have shown that many redesign efforts simply do not deliver their intended results:

- In a detailed study of 20 corporate redesign efforts, McKinsey & Co. found that only six of the companies achieved significant financial benefits.

- A survey by the Wyatt Co. showed that 85% of respondents had instituted some form of corporate restructuring to improve profitability. After two years, costs had failed to decline in 46% of the cases and, in several instances, had even risen. Additionally, 58% of respondents had sought to increase productivity, but only a third had done so.

- Of 600 companies responding to a CSC Index survey, a mere 39% reported that their "redesign" effort had met most of their goals.

The principal reason that expectations for redesign often are not met is that it is treated as an end, rather than as a means to the end of refocusing on customers through fundamental change in an organization's culture. Rather, the two challenges faced are: (1) how to develop a customer- and sales-driven focus that can compete effectively with highly sophisticated marketers for whom meeting customer needs is the number one objective, and (2) how to fundamentally change the culture of their institutions to meet this new world of competition.

From this broader perspective, real redesign can be seen for what it is: a catalytic event (taking 6 months or so to design and 12 to 18 months to implement) in a 5- to 10-year process of change that leads to (1) a fundamental refocusing from internal issues to external customer service and (2) a revitalization of culture, from sleepy and often autocratic to dynamic and empowering. A successful redesign contributes to such customer focus and cultural change, and only then, as a by-product, does it result in a significant economic benefit that is sustainable (rather than being a short-term gratification for stock analysts).

One example is U.S. Bancorp, whose stock price has increased 794%, ROE has improved from 11% to 23%, and efficiency ratio (cents of cost to regenerate each dollar of revenue) has declined from 63% to 44% since it began to redesign in August 1992. Such dramatic improvements are not just the result of redesign; rather, they came about because the organization's leaders and employees used its redesign as a springboard for customer focus and to help transform their culture into an entrepreneurial, sales-driven engine.

EXHIBIT 1   Stock Market Rewards "Real" Redesign*

U.S. Bancorp (Formerly Star Banc)

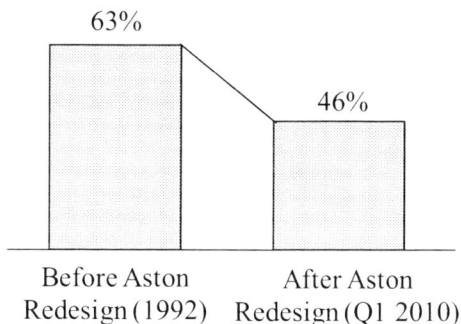

63%

46%

Before Aston
Redesign (1992)

After Aston
Redesign (Q1 2010)

Efficiency Ratio

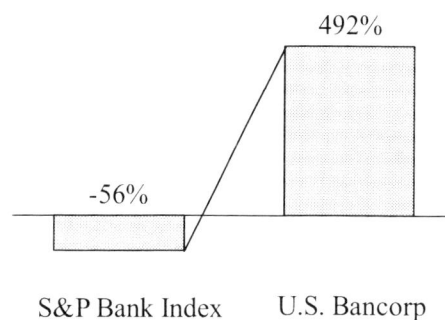

492%

-56%

S&P Bank Index

U.S. Bancorp

**Stock Price Appreciation Since
Redesign (1992 - June, 2010)**

* Note: updated since date of article's publication

What is an Organization's Culture?

"Culture" can be very broadly defined as the shared patterns of employees' values, attitudes, and behaviors, and employees' characteristic way of perceiving the organization's norms and roles. The culture is determined by employees' experience of the organization's shared history and their response to external and internal environmental influences as reflected through their common values, attitudes, and behaviors.

Values are the individual's sense of what ought to be, as opposed to what is. When a group faces a new project, issue, or problem, the first solutions are driven by such values because a shared basis for determining what is factual or real has not yet, by definition, been determined. Group members state a solution based on their convictions.

An *attitude* is the individual's reflection of what he or she feels. Employees who highly value their personal life, for instance, when told they have to work on a project over the weekend, show that they do not feel like it.

A *behavior* is the individual's demonstration of what he or she "wants to do" or how he or she thinks it is wise to act in order to be rewarded. Different from values and attitudes, behaviors can change relatively quickly to reflect new environmental forces. If a new boss is a stickler for punctuality, employees start turning up for meetings on time.

Culture is in a constant state of evolution; the pressures for greater and greater cultural adaptation are mounting, but the barriers to adaptation are significant.

How Does Culture Change?

An organization's culture evolves in three stages (see Exhibit 2). Take the example of a theoretical bank founded in 1980 that has grown to more than $20 billion in assets today. As employees were hired over the first 10 years, the culture gelled. Its development was driven by (1) getting the organization team to "buy into" a configuration of new values, attitudes, and behaviors; (2) recruiting and socializing with new employees to familiarize them with and have them adopt the bank's values, attitudes and behaviors; and (3) living with the bank's shared history, beliefs, and assumptions.

EXHIBIT 2 Stages of Culture Change

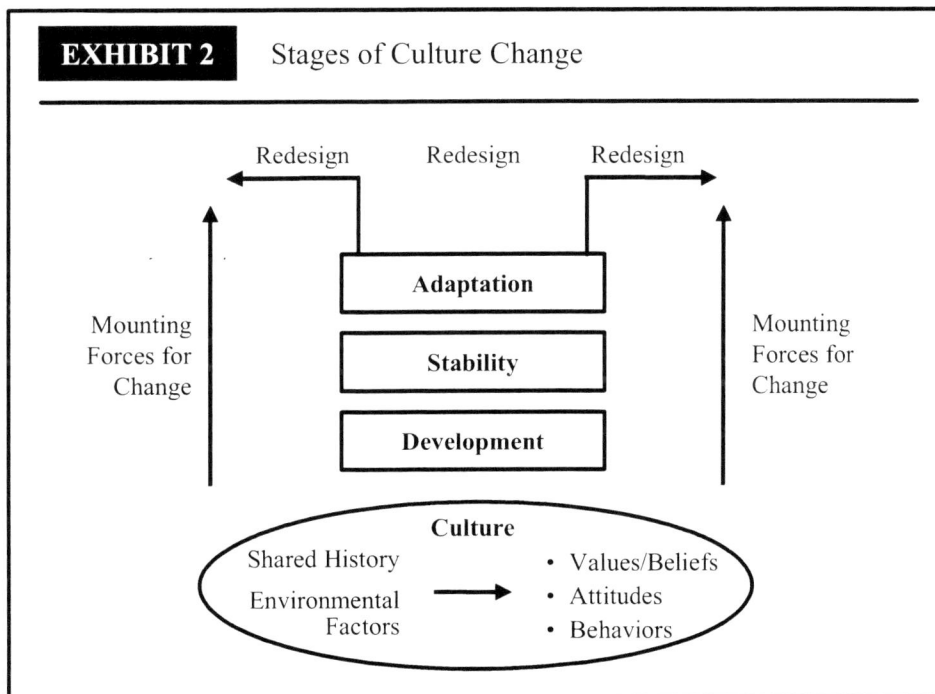

From 1990 to 2000, a period of stability led to (1) a comfortable environment ("we've been doing it this way for years"; "we don't need to change"; "we're doing okay"); (2) the development of counter cultures that did not accept the dominant organization's culture; and yet (3) the constant reaffirmation of the core culture through promotions, bonuses, and other incentives.

The rapid interest rate shifts of the early 2000s led to an inevitable need for adaptation in order to survive margin pressures. A survival mentality undermined the earlier stability and people began to succeed as a result of the flexibility they demonstrated.

A new CEO and top management team recognized that such reactive adaptation was no longer enough. They are seeking to redesign the bank's culture. This, they acknowledge, will take years to achieve. (See Exhibit 3 for a simple assessment form of where the organization stands in this dynamic cultural progression.)

EXHIBIT 3

Do you face environmental issues?
- Are customers satisfied with the speed with which the bank responds to their changing needs?
- Are fewer promotions available because of "middle age spread"?
- Are you considering "virtual" technology solutions, with the dis-aggregation of low-value processing to outsourcers and the dispersing of operations tasks to remote, client/server platforms?

Where are you in the stages of culture?

Development
- Does the organization have a clear identity and role?
- Does senior management know what the bank's core mission is?
- Is it hard to state specifically what values, attitudes and behaviors are shared across the bank?

Stability
- Have you developed shared values, attitudes and behaviors?
- Is there a feeling of complacency and well-being?
- Do you like who you are?

Adaptation
- Is senior management reacting to internal and external challenges on an ad hoc basis?
- Is technology changing more quickly than you are?

Redesign
- Is senior management consciously challenging the status quo?
- Does senior management have a vision of what the new bank should be?
- Is senior management ready to take the risk of proactive change?

Why the Need for Such Proactive, Fundamental Redesign of Culture?

The world is changing so fast that reaction is not enough. Organizations must meet such forces of change as the potential, through advanced, distributed technology, for a smaller, more dispersed work force and the aging baby boomers. The resulting middle-age "spread" will mean ever-increasing competition for high-level organizational positions. In addition, the traditional lure of promotion as an incentive for motivation and commitment may therefore be threatened, creating a need to consider alternate ways to keep employees involved and productive.

Why Redesign Now?

The top reasons why senior managers believe they face a redesign imperative are as follows:

- Employees often spend more than 60% of their working day focused on controls and other inward-oriented processes, rather than on customer sales and service.

- Employees know that many of their daily responsibilities are pointless and do not contribute to customer value.

- Top management is insulated from customers by excessive layers of management.

- The stock price is too weak to defend against unwanted takeover bids or trades at a market discount, barring the use of stock as an acquisition currency.

- Excessive redundancy of processes is obvious.

- Staff groups in line areas have multiplied.

- Cost and/or revenue efficiencies from previous acquisitions are not achieved between 12 and 18 months after the acquisition, if at all.

- Technological investments do not result in either significant cost savings or revenue enhancements.

- Pricing is driven not by the value customers perceive they receive, but by what competitors charge.

Will Organizations Accept Cultural Change?

Although people are resistant to change, if employees, suppliers, and customers regard the CEO and senior management as committed to and clear about the values and mission of the new organization and view their actions as consistent with the required changes in behavior, they will support efforts to change culture. However, barriers to cultural change will often arise, such as:

- Management changing what it says it wants in behaviors but not the systems for reward and recognition.

- Employees viewing the changes as just a "project" that will end, therefore requiring them to play along for now (i.e., "This too shall pass").

- Members of counter cultures (supportable during the era of stability) becoming guerrillas against change.

In this context of cultural challenges, what is "real" redesign and how can it support the creation of a new culture driven by customer focus? "Real" redesign is the fundamental redesign, from a blank sheet of paper, of an organization's processes (chains of tasks leading to an output for an internal or external customer's value), along with re-pricing to reflect customer value.

Barriers to Redesign

Even when an organization's board and management have decided on a design to refocus on the customer and to assist in establishing a new culture, significant barriers to change arise. These include:

- Cost and productivity goals dominating or supplanting customer and cultural priorities. If a "redesign" is driven solely or principally by cost reduction, it will inevitably become (despite whatever good intentions underlie the effort) a "slash and burn" destroyer of employee loyalty and commitment, customer franchise, and medium- and long-term corporate health and stock price.

- Short-term focus on the intensive redesign experience dominating the long-term cultural and employee health of the organization. The focus from day one has to be on "re-recruiting" employees after the redesign has been implemented. Management must give them a vision why redesign is necessary in order to create a long-term future of success and personal fulfillment. Otherwise, restructuring is simply a sacrifice of employees for the sake of stock analysts' greed. And it will not work.

Attempting to Redesign Slices of the Organization in Successive Waves

Many "redesign" efforts are carried out as a rolling optimization of particular processes (e.g., hiring, financial planning) or lines of business and functions (e.g., financial services, systems, and operations) over several years. This leads to organizational catharsis as (1) successive waves of employee layoffs or redeployment occur and (2) continuous interruptions of customer relationships result from successive process discontinuities. The rolling approach just does not work.

How Can Redesign Play Its Proper Catalytic Role?

To briefly summarize the "to do's" of successful redesign that can overcome the barriers to change, boards, chairpersons, and CEOs should:

- Acknowledge that redesign is a means to an end. You must be committed to painting a bigger picture of cultural change and customer focus and be prepared to dedicate yourselves to realizing it.

- Understand that redesign is about organizational revitalization rather than just redesigning cost processes, systems, and structures, or establishing pricing discipline and outward focus. It is about the management of change.

- Meet four organizational imperatives for successful redesign:

  - ***Demonstrate a commitment to change.*** Place the redesign properly in the context of broader cultural change and customer focus. Make it a top priority. And involve yourself, senior management, a dedicated change team, and every employee in the redesign.

  - ***Demonstrate a commitment to fairness.*** Design the process so that everyone perceives that all areas of the organization are being reviewed. There must be no sacred cows. Nor should there be special ways of looking at high-growth, strategically critical, or "pet" units. In addition, develop a human resources strategy to let employees know in advance that they will be treated in an equitable, generous, supportive and caring fashion.

— ***Demonstrate a commitment to involvement.*** Management must design a creative program to continuously communicate to employees in an honest and open fashion, through multiple, diverse channels (most importantly, continuous, face-to-face, informal access, not just a newsletter). And you must create a multifaceted approach to allowing each employee a voice in the redesign process (combining low-risk group brainstorming, a change idea hotline, anonymous and attributed suggestion sheets, and so forth). This will enable staff members to truly sense that their contributions are valued.

— ***Demonstrate a commitment from day one to the "new organization."*** Nothing should start until the roadmap for cultural change and re-recruitment of employees is in place. Reassuring staff up-front that the redesign is a well-conceived, deliberate, far-sighted effort to position the organization for long-term preeminence and employee self-fulfillment will help win the heads and hearts of all constituencies.

All of these guidelines may sound Pollyanish and naive; of course, redesign will cause uncertainty, anxiety, and pain. But employees can show an untapped energy for change if they see that (1) redesign is a measured response to the competitive environment; (2) senior management is totally committed to making it work on a clear, livable time frame (not as the latest of a series of knee-jerk cost reduction exercises); and (3) it is based on fairness and openness.

So-called redesign efforts will continue to fail if they are treated as an end, rather than a means to cultural revitalization. Such failure comes at a high price in terms of breaching the covenant with loyal employees and failing to satisfy customer value expectations. Managers do face an imperative to change, but they must be accountable for making that change happen effectively in pursuit of a clear vision of a culture that will foster future success.

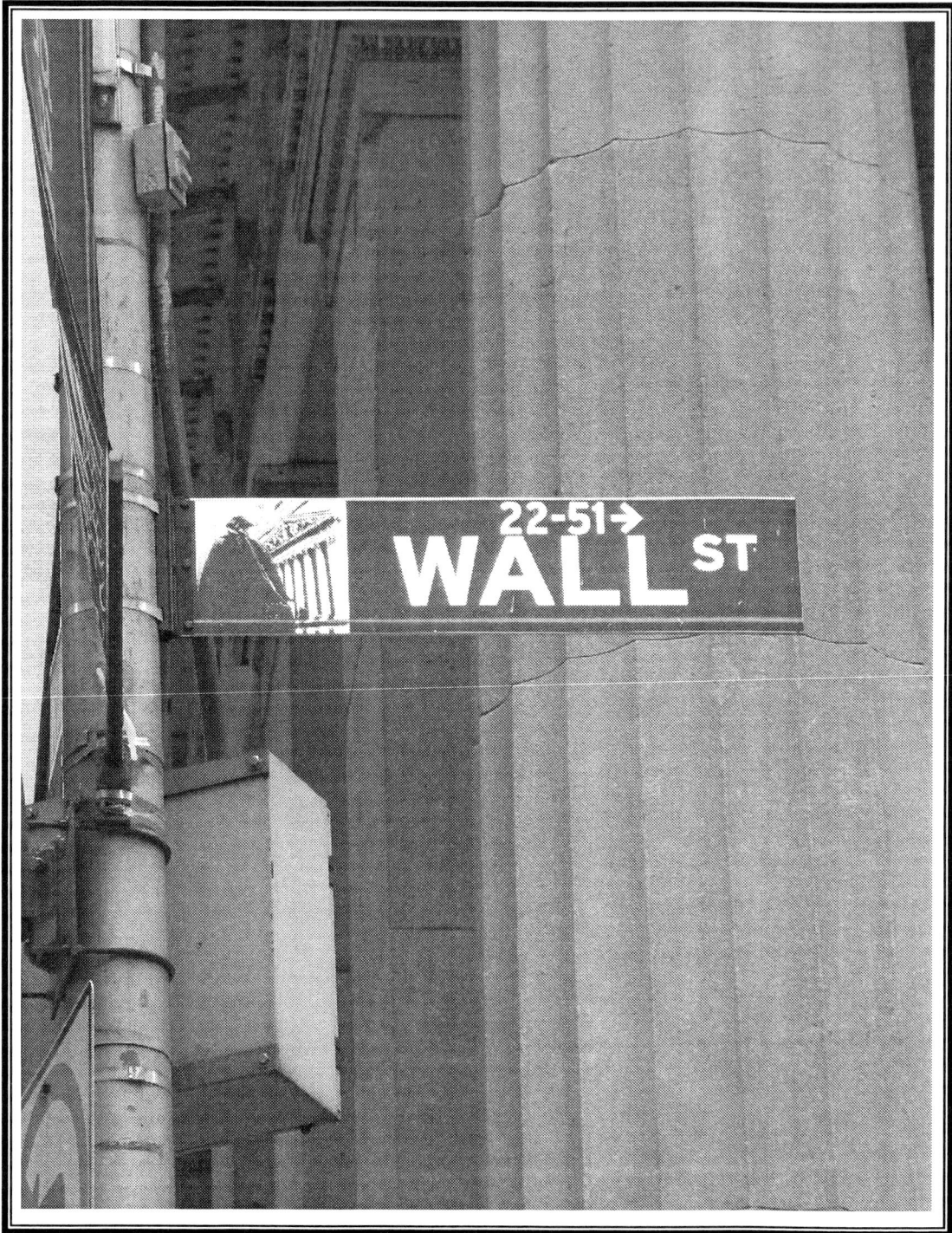

CASE STUDIES

First Niagara Financial Group

From 2003—2004, Aston led a strategic design at First Niagara Financial Group that focused on honing First Niagara's strategy as they moved through their transition from a mutual savings bank to a publicly traded financial services institution. Putting the customer at the forefront of their approach, First Niagara has made outstanding progress since implementation and continues to reward shareholders through solid growth and financial performance.

Aston's focused approach supported First Niagara's efforts to grow assets by 114% in sixteen months to become an $8 billion regional bank in 2005. EPS increased by 29% from 3rd quarter 2004 to 3rd quarter 2005 and efficiency ratio improved from 58% to 54% in the same timeframe.

Total Assets:
Growth Since Inception of Partnership
(2003 – 2010)

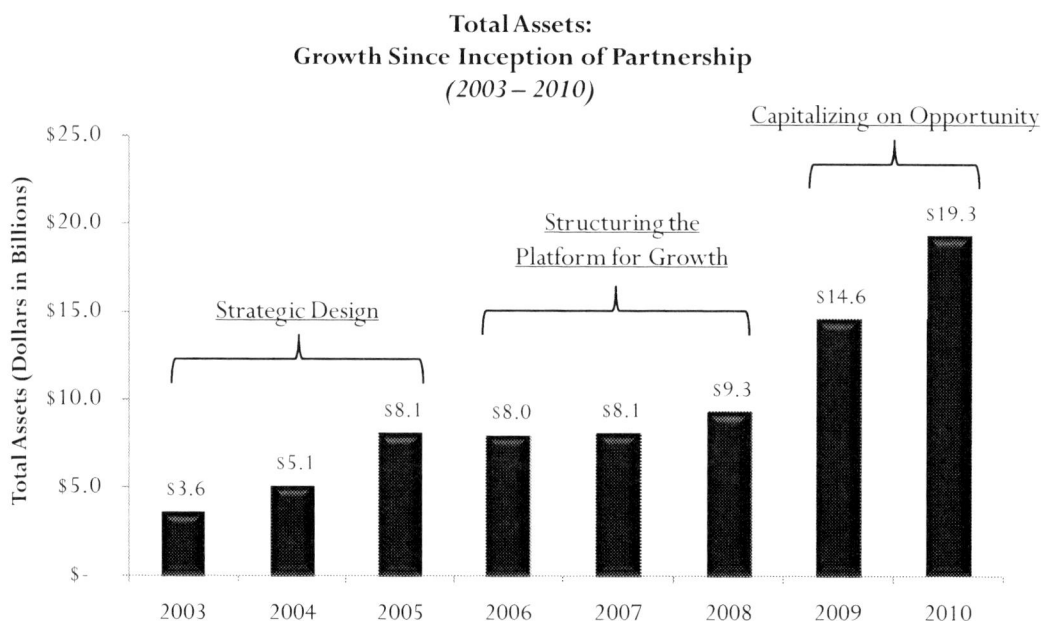

After working with Aston through two transformative acquisitions and the development of a well structured and scalable platform for growth, First Niagara has continued to grow to a $20 billion company and has delivered 46% total shareholder return since Aston's work began in 2003, approximately triple the return of the thrift index.

First Niagara is in excellent position to continue outperforming the overall market and is rated "buy" or "strong buy" by six of eight analysts covering the stock.

Return on Average Assets

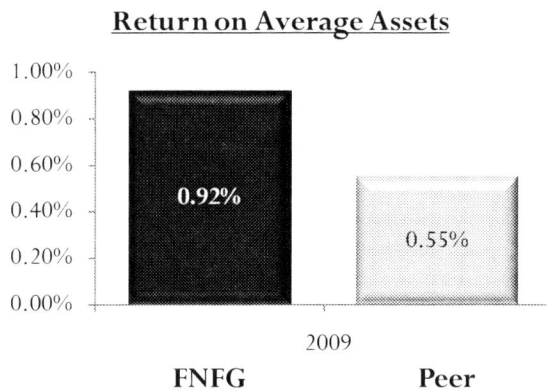

FNFG: 0.92% Peer: 0.55% (2009)

TCE/TA

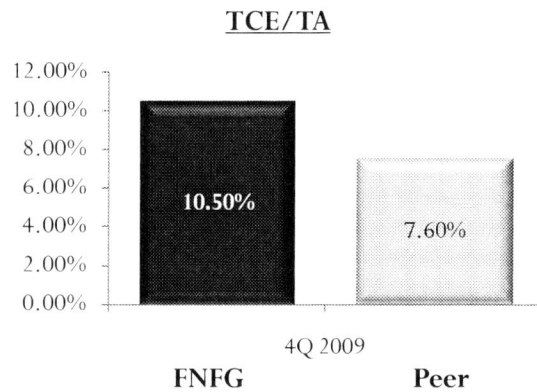

FNFG: 10.50% Peer: 7.60% (4Q 2009)

NPLs/Total Loans

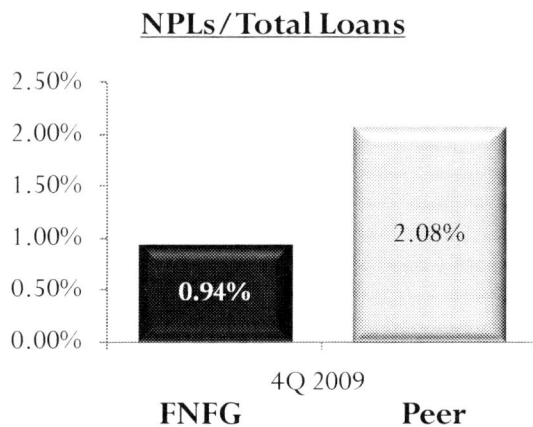

FNFG: 0.94% Peer: 2.08% (4Q 2009)

NCOs/Average Loans

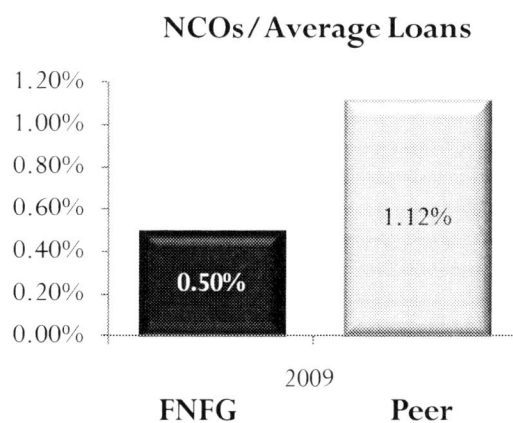

FNFG: 0.50% Peer: 1.12% (2009)

U.S. Bancorp (formerly StarBanc)

When we began our work with StarBanc in 1992, it was their goal to grow into **a US financial services leader** and avoid a "bear hug" bid from Fifth Third. Through a hugely successful design, outstanding ongoing management and a series of well-timed strategic acquisitions (the most notable being Firstar in 1998 and then U.S. Bancorp in 2000) their asset growth has been phenomenal:

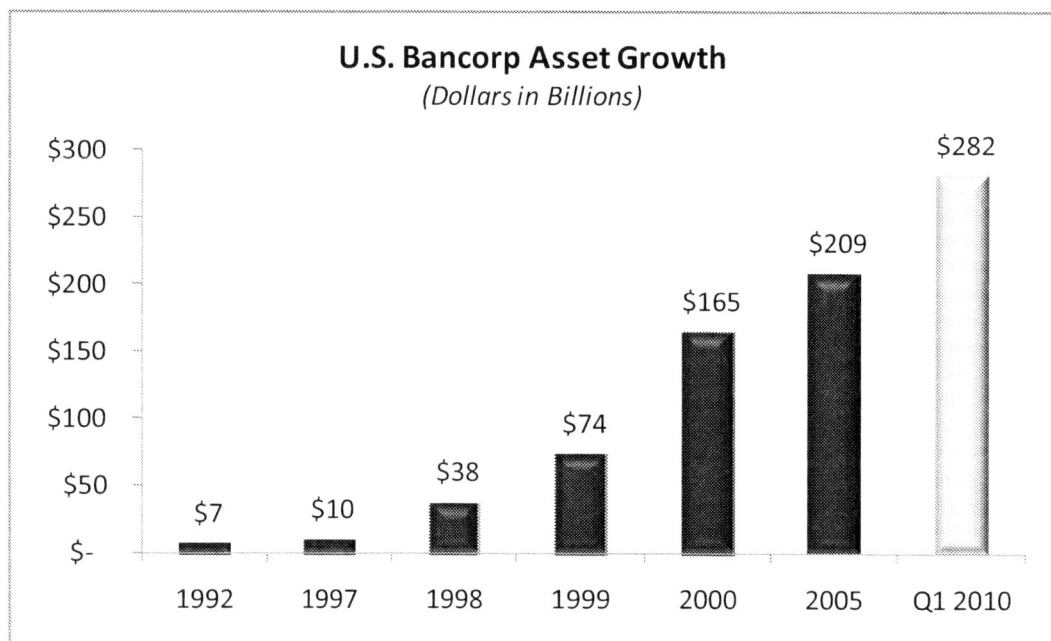

U.S. Bancorp Asset Growth
(Dollars in Billions)

1992	$7
1997	$10
1998	$38
1999	$74
2000	$165
2005	$209
Q1 2010	$282

Key to their success has been Jerry Grundhofer's team's systematic integration of acquired organizations, including careful expense management and special consideration of customer service and satisfaction along the way. These initiatives have led to continually improving efficiency ratios (from 63% to 46%) and their exceptional customer service, encapsulated in their nationally recognized 5-Star Service Guarantees:

Five "Core" Service Guarantees

- US Bank 24-Hour Bankers will be available 24 hours a day, 7 days a week.
- ATMs will be available 24 hours a day, 7 days a week.
- You will wait no longer than 5 minutes in any teller line.
- We will respond to all questions the same day, when asked before 3 p.m.
- Checking and savings statements will always be accurate.

As a result, they have been able to deliver **outstanding returns to shareholders**, with their stock price having risen over 492% since 1992 (compared to a 56% decline in the S&P Bank Index over the same period). Total shareholder return over the same period (including dividend reinvestment) has been 963%, or 27% per year.

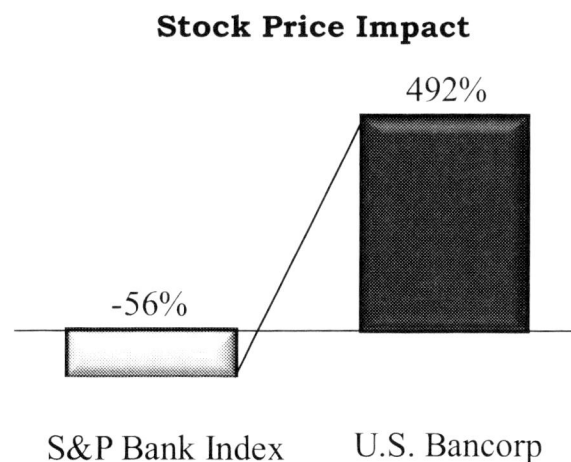

Stock Price Impact

492%

-56%

S&P Bank Index   U.S. Bancorp

**Stock Price Appreciation Since
Redesign (1992 - June, 2010)**

St. George Bank (Australia)

St. George Bank was facing takeover speculation in early 2000 and was looking to build a new strategy around a "Best Bank" concept. This concept focused on completing post-integration efforts effectively, and becoming the best in the business on the fundamentals of customer service, high-value customer retention and product cross-sell. They succeeded in staving off a takeover bid and continue to thrive.

As they looked to grow, they also felt they had to operate "leaner" and more efficiently. Careful examination of **operating processes** and a series of resulting improvement initiatives saw their **cost to income ratio improve from 58% down to 46%**.

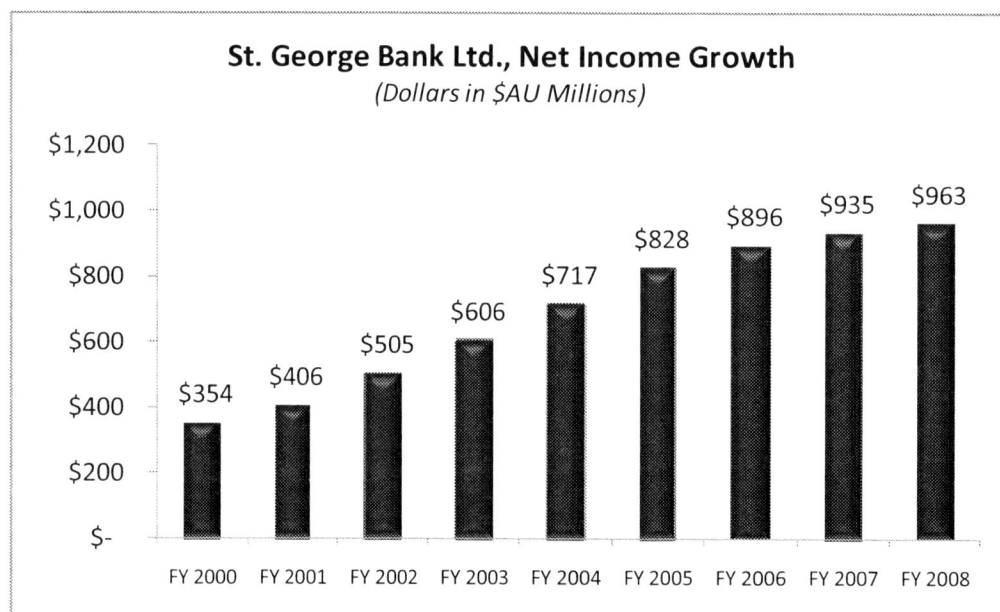

St. George Bank Ltd., Net Income Growth
(Dollars in $AU Millions)

FY 2000	FY 2001	FY 2002	FY 2003	FY 2004	FY 2005	FY 2006	FY 2007	FY 2008
$354	$406	$505	$606	$717	$828	$896	$935	$963

St. George Bank was acquired by Westpac Banking Corporation in December, 2008.

They also looked to **customer service** as a key to differentiating themselves from their much larger competitors. As a result, customer satisfaction has risen dramatically and their **retention rates for high-value customers** has also climbed to an impressive level.

This has led to steady and substantial stock price growth since design (increase of 186%, or 235% including dividend reinvestment), compared to the overall Australian market index of 38% from August 2000 to December 2008.

Customer Satisfaction

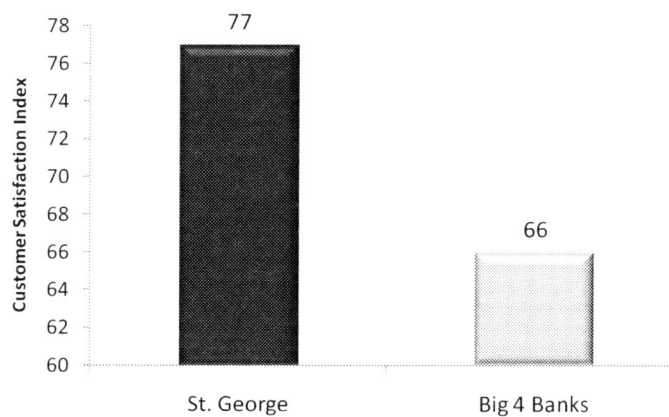

Customer Retention

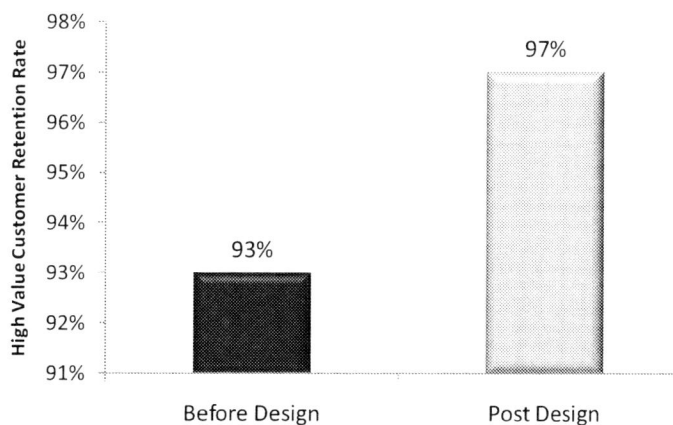

First Security

In 1995, First Security faced **major operational hurdles** as a result of several recent acquisitions and was looking to define its strategic direction. Already a leading presence in the Inter-Mountain West, the emerging strategy **focused on maximizing its brand and franchise value** by creating an integrated financial services provider capable of meeting all of its customer needs. The translation of the identified strategic objectives led to the strong growth of the franchise culminating in the successful merger with Wells Fargo in 2000.

Efficiency Ratio

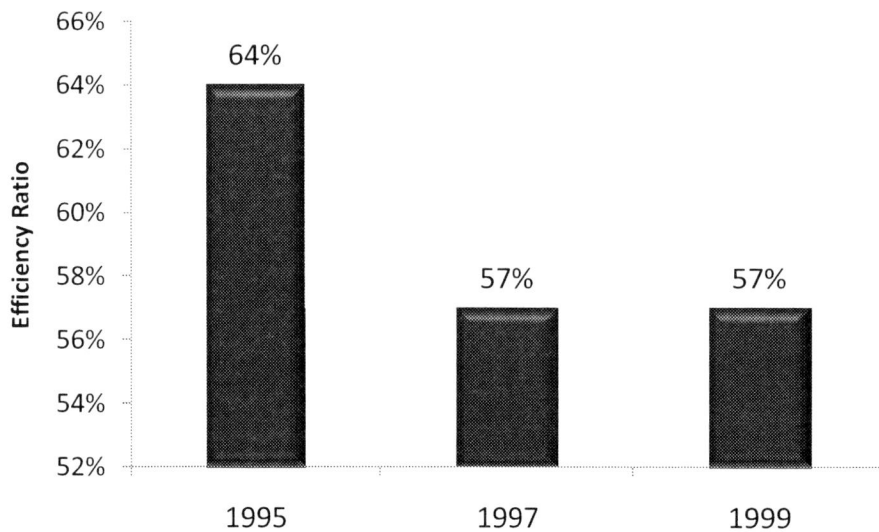

Year	Efficiency Ratio
1995	64%
1997	57%
1999	57%

Specific initiatives that underpinned their success included the **integration of their systems and call center platforms**, integrated delivery of insurance and wealth management services, and **matching service delivery to customer needs** in their expansive retail network.

Stock Price Impact

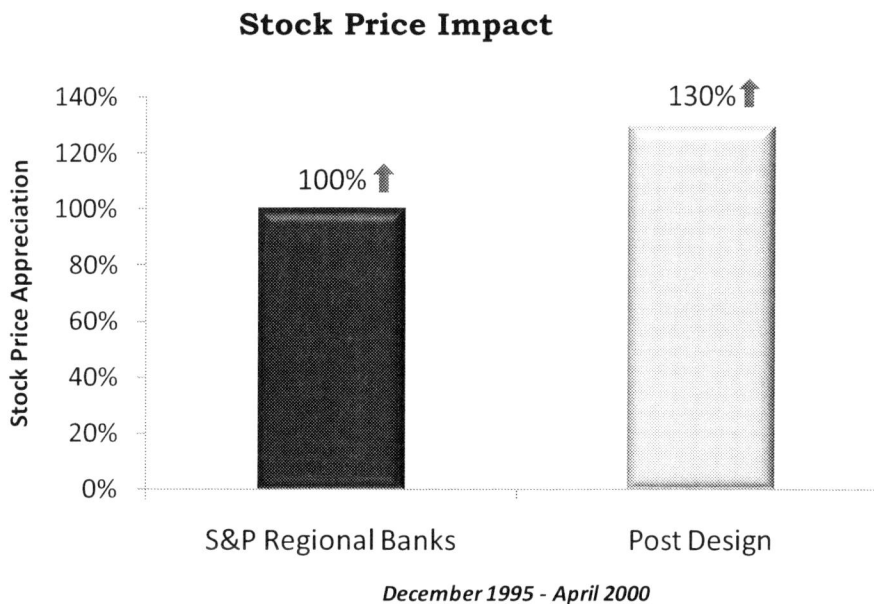

December 1995 - April 2000

Efficient operations across the organization led to increased profitability, creating average annual **EPS growth of 19%,** annual **net income growth of 22%,** and an **increase in the stock price of 130%** until their merger announcement. Over the same period, total shareholder return (including dividend reinvestment) was 197%, or 24% per year.

Signet

Aston's design partnership with **Signet Financial Corporation** followed the spin-off of the most successful national credit card company: Capital One (formerly a division within Signet). The design applied the Capital One division model as a blueprint for Signet's corporate-wide operating platform by driving a superior, sophisticated "Information Based Strategy" and building a strong performance culture to support this strategy:

- Sophisticated segment-driven products and price offerings;

- Integrated sales and service platform to support national phone and web-based delivery model;

- Superior value proposition nationally and to all bands of the market by matching demographic and credit history data, perceived needs and product offerings;

- Broad-based experimentation with new concepts using sophisticated data-warehouse (e.g., targeted home equity products with multiple test cells);

- Extensive testing applied to people management processes including recruiting, training and performance management.

Stock Price Impact

Stock Price Appreciation (y-axis, 0%–100%)

50% ↑ — S&P Bank Index

95% ↑ — Post Design

September 1996 - July 1997

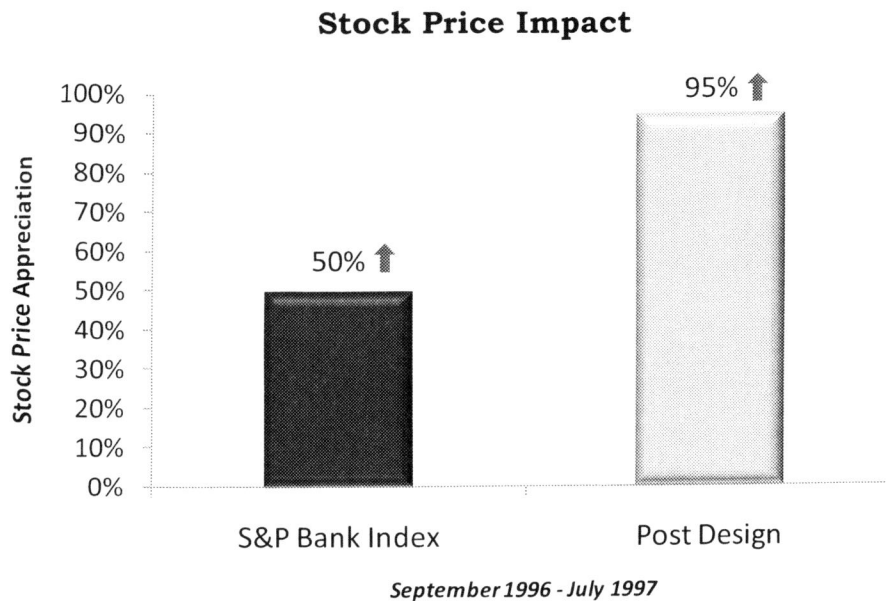

Impressive Financial Impact

- Following the announcement of design results, Signet's stock price jumped 45% in the first month (including dividend reinvestment, total return was 104% at the time of the merger)

- Efficiency ratio declined from 65 percent to 53 percent

- Revenue impact of $20 million and process cost reduction of $78 million

- Acquired by First Union Corporation in July 1997 at 3.5 times book value

Bank of Hawaii

Starting in 1999, Aston joined forces with Bank of Hawaii to design operations and re-focus strategy from a broad pan-Pacific approach to a concentrated approach focusing on core markets in Hawaii and West Pacific.

The New Era design implemented through 1999 and 2000 resulted in an increase of revenues of $46 million and operating inefficiencies reduced by $47 million and enabled Bank of Hawaii to restructure its loan portfolio and geographic footprint. Throughout 2001, Aston helped in the divestment of Bank of Hawaii's South Pacific operations to ANZ and French Territory operations to Caisse Nationale des Caisses d'Epargne. **The Bank's stock price has increased 163% since announcement of design vs. an overall market decrease of 56% in the comparable period.** Including dividend reinvestment, total shareholder return has been over 280%, more than 26% per year.

Stock Price Impact

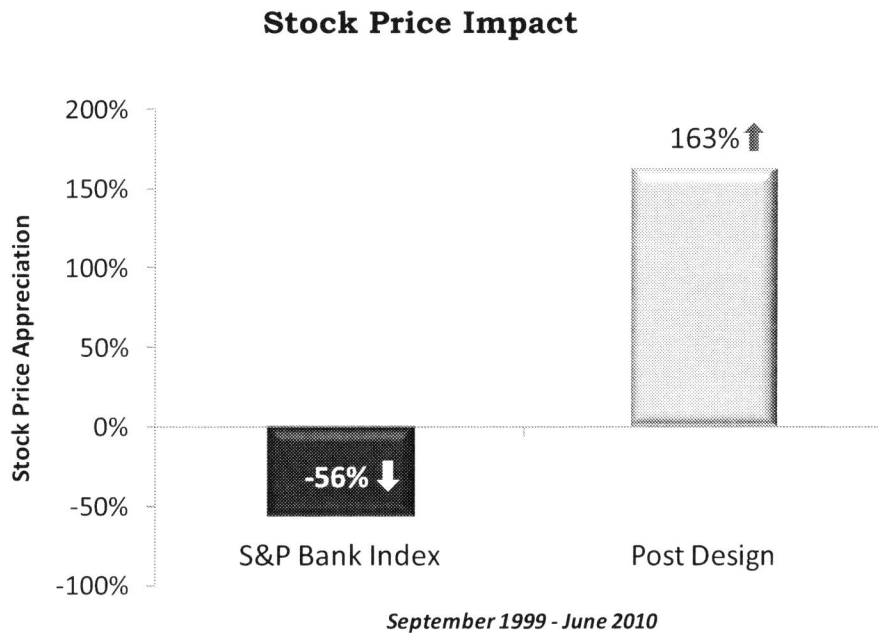

September 1999 - June 2010

Specific initiatives that underpinned Bank of Hawaii's success included **differentiating of the retail branch network**, **segmentation** and dedicated offerings to the small business customers and the **refinement of the trust and private banking sales and service platform**. By reflecting **customer value in interest-based and non-interest pricing**, Bank of Hawaii was able to both deepen share of wallet and increase profitability dramatically.

BankBoston

In 1997, BankBoston was looking to improve its customer focus as it was struggling to reposition itself after intense acquisition activity in the greater Boston market.

The design partnership focused on identifying major re-investment opportunities where revenue growth opportunities appeared most promising. The results of design quickly emerged throughout BankBoston's business lines as exemplified by **key process indicators** in the Regional Bank and underlay the merger with Fleet:

- Quality of work coming from the Retail Branches into Banking Operations up over 50%

- Small business loan applications being processed 3 times faster

- Systems availability reaching record highs even as volumes have grown by 30%

- Telebanking decreased customer wait times by over 70%

- Missing deposit claims down 42%

- Setup times for all types of new accounts down 57%

- Missing consumer loan payments down 70%

- Sales productivity in the Private Bank improved by 42%.

Stock Price Impact

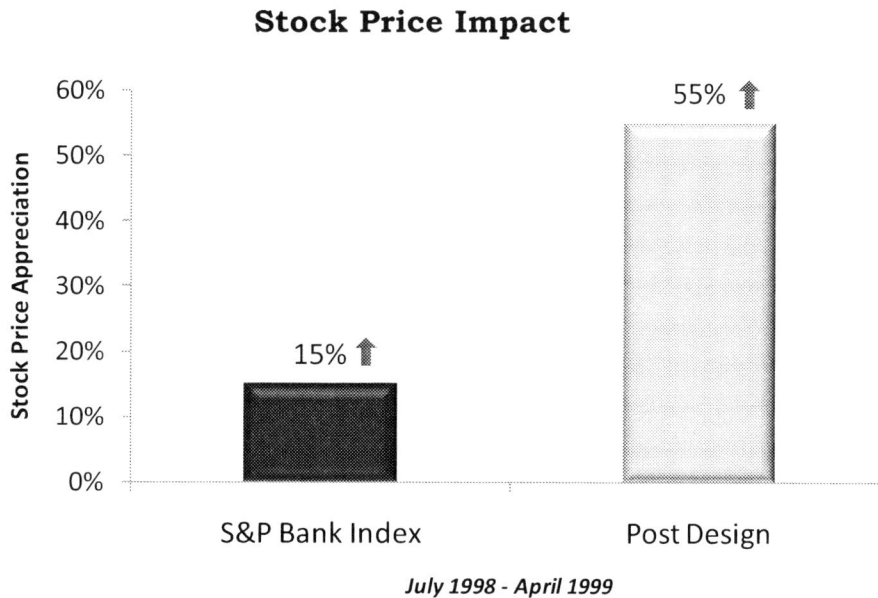

July 1998 - April 1999

Impressive Financial Impact

- ROE up from 16 to 24 percent.

- Revenue impact of $88 million and process cost reduction of $188 million.

- Stock price rose 55 percent (versus 15 percent S&P bank index). Including dividend reinvestment, total return over the period was 76 percent.

- Merger with Fleet Financial Corporation valued at $16 billion and now Bank of America.

Country Banc Holdings

Starting in 1995, Aston sponsored the formation of Country Banc Holding to **acquire, consolidate, and operate banks in Oklahoma, Kansas, and Texas.** For Country Banc's acquisition of three Oklahoma banks with combined assets of $375 million, Aston raised $50 million in common stock - $28 million invested in Country Banc and $22 million earmarked for future acquisitions.

Country **Banc went on to expand through acquisition from assets of $375 million to $600 million**, and merged into Gold Banc, a $2.7 billion Kansas holding company, in 1999.

At the time of the exit by merger, a combined institutional equity investment of $19 million was exchanged for $35 million of Gold Banc stock. Other shareholders realized $40 million.

In turn, Gold Banc was sold in November 2005 to Milwaukee-based Marshall & Ilsley for $700 million, returning a compound annual growth rate of 22% to investors.

Country Banc Holdings:

Capitalizing on profitable geographic/product niches

Annual stock price appreciation

(assuming dividend reinvestment)

% CAGR

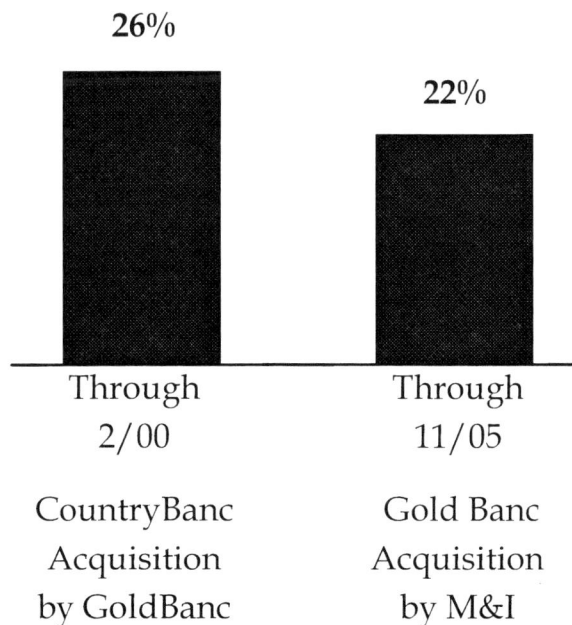

26%

22%

Through
2/00

Through
11/05

CountryBanc
Acquisition
by GoldBanc

Gold Banc
Acquisition
by M&I